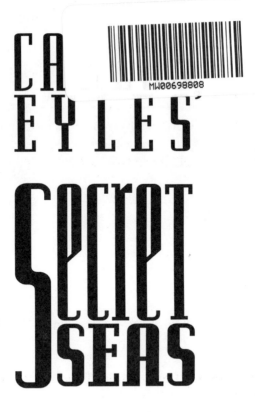

CARLOS EYLES' Secret Seas

Stories & Essays
by Carlos Eyles

Watersport Publishing, Inc.
Post Office Box 83727
San Diego, CA 92138

Printed in the USA

International Standard Book Number: 0922769-23-0

Library of Congress Catalog Card Number: 93-060326
Eyles, Carlos
        Carlos Eyles' Secret Seas

Other books by Carlos Eyles
        Diving Free
        Sea Stalking
        the Last of the Blue Water Hunters
        Sea Shadows

Cover photo by Carlos Eyles
Story and Essay illustrations by Marty James

For Margaret

Acknowledgements

There was a time when writers and artists enjoyed the support of a patron or two, generally an individual of culture with enough wealth who would sustain them until the work was produced. Patrons represent little more than a myth for me, a rumor of a bygone era. Though as an artist I have, by definition, a need for outside support. And, miraculously, I receive it. Not in the classic way of the single patron, but from a great many eager to lend a hand to a stranger. Seemingly, the more alien the stranger (me) the more generous the offering. From all corners of the globe my needs have been filled; everything from boats to clothing, food to shelter. Everyone is always gracious and supportive, encouraging me to continue to write; to bring forth a voice which reflects their personal feelings about the sea, and about the people who live in and around the sea. Quite naturally each and every one of these people have become my extended family. Theirs is the light by which these words are put down and these stories brought to life.

To attempt a list would invite omission. Those in my family know who they are. However, I would like to single out Gary Adkison of the Bahamas, and most particularly Dave and Jody Bryant of Catalina Island who have, over the years, displayed an unswerving generosity that is beyond repayment. My sincere thanks to the Bryants and Gary and to everyone who has extended themselves in my behalf.

Ken Loyst, the publisher of Watersport Publishing, Inc., probably comes closest to the definition of patron as anyone; though he could deny it. And perhaps rightly so, for he is not wealthy, by any standard of the word. But he sustains a vision, and is uncommonly generous. Often these traits get him into trouble, but in my view there are no more noble traits in man. Finally, to my wandering friend and clear-eyed critic, Jordan, who edited this work, my deep and abiding gratitude.

Carlos Eyles
winter 1992

Foreword by Michael Menduno

> *Jimmay did not answer his question, but instead asked, "Did you hear the voice of the ocean?"*
>
> *"What do you mean by the voice? Like the fish sounds in the water?" Questioned Dr. Carter.*
>
> *"No, the voice," said Jimmay patiently. "The ocean speaks. It is like a song, but sometimes like a whisper. It is felt in the high stomach, just below the chest."*
>
>
>
> Carlos Eyles,
> *Swimmer In A Secret Sea*
>

It has been a long while since author and free diver, Carlos Eyles, has published a new book of prose. Following his amazing odyssey, beginning with *The Inner Experience of Diving,* which first appeared in 1975 (and was later retitled, *Diving Free) Sea Stalking, The Last of the Blue Water Hunters,* and his black and white image book, *Sea Shadows.* Eyles' "Castaneda-esque" legacy has enthralled a generation of readers, elevating him to 'cult hero' status to those in the know.

What is it that makes Eyles' work so important? To some, it is the fact that his early books chronicle a forgotten generation of divers. Long on leg and lung, these "blue water hunters"– the fore-runners of modern scuba – opened up a new frontier for others to follow, but in the rush of technology, their legacy was almost lost. Eyles' message is in fact much more universal. Taken as a whole, his stories present a specific search for meaning, *"a spirituality that man(sic) has lost,"* and that *"bold ones spend their life seeking."* To Eyles, this power is something held in the environment, and his life and writing reflects it.

Eyles writes about a wilderness – the wilderness within each of us – as it is reflected back through the environment. Perhaps it is only by venturing out beyond the safe confines of the known – like the free diver – unencumbered, vulnerable, operating in an alien environment whose order can only be sensed through direct experience – that we can come to this place of knowledge, a place that has been largely forgotten in the twentieth century world. That's what makes Eyles' new book, *Secret Seas*, well worth the wait.

In this rich collection of fifteen original short stories and essays – some previously published, but all rewritten for this book – storyteller Eyles is once again in his element, inviting the reader to take a closer look at the unfathomable world we find ourselves inhabiting. *Secret Seas* takes us to the far corners of the heart and mind as well as the ocean's realm. Often it is the very technology civilization embraces that is Eyles' favorite antagonist. A cave on Catalina Island filled with lobsters that cannot be reached by two young divers using scuba; a dilemma with an interesting resolution in the *Lobster Museum*. *The Speargun* takes place on a remote island in Fiji, and again the specter of technology intrudes on an otherwise perfect culture. *The Bay* represents a microcosm of this same intrusion on our own shores and the inevitable price that is paid by us all in one form or another.

The characters of these stories know these impeccably, and through their eyes we are able to grasp a better understanding of it for ourselves. Such is the case for *The Education of Jubal Freemountain*, which also reads as perhaps Eyles' own spiritual journey. Eyles' essays may be thoughtful, or amusing, but always they are powerful. He is not afraid to reveal his flawed encounters with the sea, as evidenced by *The One I Wish had Got Away, The Judas Goat,* and *Tides, Currents, and Other Moving Experiences*. Stories the average diver might relate to. But here the scale is grand, the adventure is high, and the background of the Sea of Cortez is spectacular as it must have been in those early days of underwater hunting. *Swimmer in a Secret Sea* might best sum up this collection, for it travels the length and breadth of the mind as well as the world in search for the answers only to realize that some secrets are revealed in the depth of the soul. And for the soulless, life becomes a fruitless journey.

There are many layers to Eyles' work, and like the ocean itself his writings give a different view with every plunge into his unique domain.

Table of Contents

Secret Seas

Stories & Essays

by Carlos Eyles

Outboard Jack

I REMEMBER THE FIRST TIME I SAW HIM. I was fishing in my usual place on the pier and he came walking up the steep, dingy ramp with a 25-horse outboard slung over his shoulder. I never saw anyone carry a big outboard that way, and figured he was about the strongest man I'd ever seen. He was probably heading for my dad's outboard shop, the only one on the island. I reeled in my line, and ran like crazy around the mooring storage and the island store. I got to the back door of Dad's shop as he was coming through the front. My dad isn't exactly small, but standing next to this fellow, he looked shorter than I'd ever seen him. This guy was at least a foot taller, and he had a big, old beard and his hair was all mussed up, and he smiled a lot. He had real blue eyes, and they smiled more than his mouth. He and my dad got to talking, first about the motor, which had a busted water pump, then about the ocean. Dad always got around to talking about the ocean. He loved everything about it, and fished and dived it every chance he got. Dad knew all the good spots from one end of the island to the other. They kept on talking, and this fellow, his name was Jack, seemed to know every good fishing spot that my dad knew, and then some. He was a free diving spearfisherman, and you could tell he knew his way around the water. He gave Dad respect because he too was a free diver. I mean, not nearly as good as him, but it didn't matter, he treated Dad as an equal, and they got along fine.

One thing led to another, and Dad said that they were going to have this fish fry down at the beach tonight, and that he was welcome to come by. Problem was no one had come up with any fish, and it looked like it was going to be beans and a big salad, but it'd be fun anyway. Jack said, "Well how much fish are you going to need?"

Dad said, "We're going to have about a dozen or more folks – some coming from Black Point, some coming from as far away as Hen Rock, maybe sixteen if everybody shows up."

"If you loan me one of your outboards," Jack said, "maybe I can scare something up." Well, Dad gave him an old twenty-five that ran pretty good, and Jack hefted it over his shoulder and left the way he had come in. Dad said nothing, but he smiled and shook his head a little. I followed Jack clear down to the pier and out to his skiff. He knew I was following, but didn't say anything until he got to the skiff. He started hooking the engine up to the transom, then looked up and asked my name. I said it was Ricky, and I asked if those big wooden spearguns laying in the bow were his. He said they were, and asked if I would like to see them up close. I said sure, and he waved me aboard.

At one time, those guns must have been a pretty sight, all varnished up and slick looking, but now they were chewed up with scrapes and scratches, and so many nicks you couldn't count 'em all. "I'll bet these spear guns have seen a lot of fish."

"Well Rick," he said, "that's a bet you'd win hands down. They've seen more fish than would fill the hold of that trawler over there." And he pointed to old-man Hanson's fishing boat, the biggest on this side of the island.

"That'd be a lot of fish," I said.

"It is a lot of fish, Rick. Took a lot of years too. You ever think about being a diver, and getting your own food whenever you want it?"

"Yeah, I think about it all the time. My dad's pretty good with halibut, and he's starting to take me with him. I've seen a couple. Saw him spear one a couple of weeks ago. I never saw it sitting in the sand though. He pointed right down to it, and I couldn't see a thing until he speared it. Then it just took off, it was almost as big as me - not as thick, but just as wide. Have you speared any halibut?"

"Rick, I guess I've speared just about every kind of fish that's good to eat, except a broadbill. You know what a broadbill is?"

"Sure," I said, "it's a swordfish, but nobody's ever speared a broadbill. Have they?"

"Right again, Rick. Nobody's ever speared a broadbill. But I've been thinking about it. This year could be the year."

He winked at me, and his smile made me smile. He finished tightening down the engine, then plugged in the fuel line. "Let's see if this baby's got any life to her," he said. And with one arm, Jack pulled on the starter cord. He gave it three pulls, then choked it, and pulled again. She fired up.

"Untie my painter, will ya Rick. I'll see you around supper time." He idled out between the moorings to the mouth of the cove. I ran along the beach so I could see which way he headed. Jack swung west, kicking the engine up as soon as he cleared the moorings. He was out of sight in fifteen seconds.

That evening, an hour before sundown, Jack showed up again at the pier. I was waiting on the beach, and watched him pull in. He lifted two huge yellows out of the boat, and carried them down the pier and over to where my dad and some of the folks were milling around the tables, drinking beer and setting up the food. When they saw him coming no one said a word. He walked right up and said, "Where do you want these fish, Tyman?" That was my dad's name. He looked at Jack, and the two fish, that must have gone 30 pounds each.

"Hell, lay 'em down on this table, we'll fillet 'em right here. Ben, you start up the barbecue, we're going to be eating some fresh fish tonight!" Then he said, "Patty," that was my mom's name, "get this man a cold beer." Everyone was smiling and Jack took a long pull on his beer. He looked down at me and smiled and winked and said, "How ya doin' Rick?"

I couldn't think of anything to say, so I just smiled back. I noticed that everyone was looking at Jack out of the corners of their eyes, both the women and the men. No one was too sure about him, except me and my dad. About the time we sat down to supper though, he was talking and smiling with everyone. Dad had told them about how he came walking into the shop with the outboard over his shoulder, and everyone laughed and called him "Outboard Jack."

We ate until our bellies were full to busting. Everyone found their way over to Jack and thanked him for providing all that fish.

He said if he had known such a friendly gathering was having these cookouts, he'd have been making his contribution a long time ago. And they said if they had known somebody could get them this much fish, they'd a had these cookouts more often.

After that we started to have cookouts three times a week. Outboard Jack would come in with yellowtail, white sea bass, and calico, if we wanted it. My mom liked calico best, and he always brought her one. After dinner, the men sat around talking about the ocean, and the best places to find certain kinds of fish. They all knew the island like the back of their hands, but Jack knew it in a way nobody else did. He knew spots my dad didn't even know about. Of course, he was going after big yellows and whites, while most every-one else was satisfied with halibut and calico. Jack was always talking about big fish; who got the biggest back in this year and that. I think he had a couple of records of his own, but he never mentioned them.

Halfway through the summer, all the locals had heard about Jack. And they'd come down after the cookouts, nibble on the leftovers, and listen to the stories. I don't think we ever had more fun than that summer. Everybody was always ready to have a good time. Toward the end of the evening, after drinking a bunch of beers, Jack always turned the conversation around to broadbill. He would ask questions like, who was catching them, where they were catching them, and which boats were the best broadbill boats, so he could go up and ask the skippers where the action was. Nobody put two and two together until later in the summer when the broadbill were starting to make their run.

One night my dad asked him straight out, "Why are you so interested in broadbill, Jack?"

Jack looked him right in the eye and said, "Cause I want to spear one Tyman, that's why I'm so interested."

"Hell, nobody's ever speared a broadbill."

"That's why I want to do it, Tyman, 'cause it's never been done." '

My dad looked at him cold, and said, "You know why it's never been done? Because that's the meanest, toughest, most dangerous fish that lives in the sea, bar none. Hell, a broadbill sank a boat here about four years ago. Rammed it and started thrashing around until it tore the planking loose from the side of the boat and sank it. Them broadbill have leapt right into a boat's cockpit after the harpooners – killed a man on the east end ten years ago. Got him right through the chest, then somehow jumped back into the water and got away clean. Go look in the bar, there's a broadbill spike sticking right through a three-inch oak plank. Hell, you couldn't drive a nail that big through a piece of wood like that if you had all day."

All the time my dad was talking, Jack was smiling his smile, his blue eyes dancing. When Dad was through giving him all the reasons why he shouldn't even be thinking about spearing a broadbill, Jack said, "I figure we'll need about five hundred feet of thousand-pound-test line, and maybe three of those big red tugboat fenders to slow it down. Then of course, we'll have to get us a regular broadbill boat with a high tower so we can spot 'em in the water. We can have the plank out so I can slip overboard and put a spear into it before it knows what hit it. Then scramble back to the boat, and let it tire itself out on all that flotation.

My dad just looked at him, so did Dave and Ben and Bill. They all just looked at Jack like he was crazy. And Jack kept right on smiling. Finally he said, "It'll be fun. Everyone can come along, and help split the cost of the boat. You can bring Rick along. If nothing else, we'll have a hell of a fine day."

Then everyone started to smile and laugh and say, "Why not? We can always troll for tuna or something." Everyone except my dad, he didn't smile at all.

It took Jack about a week to get all the rigging he needed. He had to make a couple of trips to the mainland for the line and the big red buoys. We had reports that the harpooners were getting broadbill pretty regular off the west end, about eight miles out. The time was right. Bill found us a plank boat, and we were all set to shove off the next morning. Late in the afternoon, Jack stopped by the outboard shop to check up on some last minute details with Dad. I was there when he came in. "How ya doin' Rick; how's your dad this afternoon?" And he winked at me and smiled. "You all set for the big day tomorrow?"

He had me smiling and I said, "Yeah, I'm ready." And I looked over to Dad expecting him to be sort of excited, but he was real serious.

He said, "Jack, I wish to hell you weren't doing this. Anything could happen; you know that. A fish like that can swim 30 knots, probably more. A line could catch you and take you down so fast you'd never make it back to the top. Never mind if it decided to turn on you like it does to fishermen. Why, it'd cut you to ribbons. Those fish are averaging close to a thousand pounds off the west end - you wouldn't have a chance in hell. We couldn't do a thing for you up in the boat."

"I appreciate your concern Tyman, but I believe I got this all worked out. You're right, the important thing is to stay clear of the line. That mother is going to be whipping about something fierce. Soon as I take the shot, I'll bail out on the opposite side the fish is heading. Then I'll get back to the boat as quick as I can. We can hang a knotted line up front, on the opposite side the line is fed out, and the boys can haul me up. Hell, we probably won't even see a swordfish. You know how that can be. You've done your share of broadbilling."

"Yeah, I've seen enough of them, and for your sake Jack, I pray we don't see any tomorrow."

The next morning was bright and clear, not a cloud in the sky. Jack picked us up in his skiff, and had to make six trips to the plank boat to load up all the people and gear. We headed for the west end, and got there around nine. About a mile offshore we starting taking turns up in the tower looking for a broadbill basking on the surface. Dave went up first and spent a half hour, then Bill joined him. When they came down, they said it was hard staring out at the shimmering water – your eyes got to hurtin' after awhile. The morning was the best time to look before the wind came up and raised a chop. When Ben came down, it was my dad's turn, and he took me up to the tower with him. I couldn't believe how high we were. The boat was rockin' and I got scared. Dad said to relax and I'd get used to it. Before long, I forgot about it and was just looking out across the ocean. Dad said to look for a slight break in the glass of the surface.

At first it was fun, then it got to be work. You'd strain so hard to find something that pretty soon your eyes started aching. We were about ready to come down when I thought I saw something off the left and pointed without saying a word. Dad looked, and sure enough, it was a broadbill. He yelled down, "Big fish to the south-east." Everyone on deck started running around, trying to see. We climbed down when the skipper got a fix on the fish and started moving toward it real slow.

Jack was ready to go when we got down. He had on his wetsuit and his big wooden speargun was already cocked. All that line was coiled neatly on the port side of the boat. Everyone came by and gave him a pat on the back, but didn't say anything. I started feeling sick; I was so nervous. Dad was the only one who talked to him. He said,

"Don't forget that line Jack, get clear of that line."

Jack nodded, looked at me and smiled. He gave me a thumbs up. The skipper called out, "Fifty yards," then "forty, thirty, twenty." The boat stopped and Jack slipped into the water. Everyone watched off the starboard bow. He swam toward the fish until he was about 40 feet away, then made his dive. About ten seconds later the fish exploded taking line like a runaway freight train. They all waited for Jack to pop up, but he didn't. The fish kept taking the line until it was gone, and all the floats were released. Still there was no sign of Jack.

We tracked the buoys into early afternoon, then began hauling them in. The skipper had called the Coast Guard to report a missing man. They came out with their helicopter, but I knew they wouldn't find him. When all the line was hauled up, Dad spotted a brown stain about thirty feet from the end of the bent spearshaft. The fish had got off. Dad held the line in his hand and said, "Must have wrapped around an ankle or arm and took him down."

I cried most of the way back. Jack just seemed too big to die. I couldn't see how anything in the sea could kill him, not even a broadbill. Dad said I was right. "It wasn't the sea that killed him, it was himself. He went after that broadbill for all the wrong reasons. There was no need for it. It's one thing to feed yourself and your friends, and it's another to kill something just for bragging rights. Jack was wrong in that, and it killed him."

They never did find Outboard Jack. I don't think he's dead. He was a strong swimmer, he could have made it to the mainland. Probably got picked up by a boat or something. Probably said the hell with it, I've had enough of the sea. I don't expect to see him. But every summer when the whites and yellows start running, I look for him anyway. He'll probably show up one of these days when I least expect it.

The Judas Goat

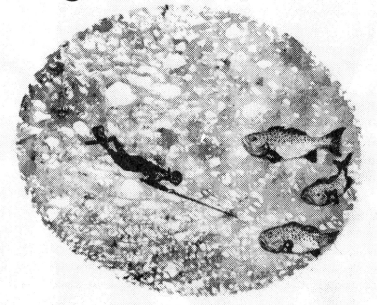

B AJA CALIFORNIA AND THE SEA OF CORTEZ were still very much
an untamed territory in 1968. The paved road wouldn't be
connected for another four years, and the coastline along the Sea of
Cortez, (what we came to call the Gulf), and its offshore islands,
were the stuff of tall tales and dreams. Guardian Angel, that fabled
island out in the middle of the Gulf, up near the Mid-riff, was perhaps the wildest dream of them all. In 1967 two major expeditions
had been launched to reach what was virtually inaccessible other
than by boat, ninety miles from San Felipe, or if one was inclined
toward disaster, by road via Bay of Los Angeles, then across the
channel to the island. Either way there was risk because the size of
the boat, which had to be large enough to cross a volatile strait of
water, was limited in size and weight by virtue of two mountain
ranges which had to be scaled by truck or car to reach San Felipe,
(unless one had the resources to hire a suitable diesel truck capable
of towing such a boat to San Felipe, and usually those with that kind
of money were not so foolish with it). There were no such mountains
to cross to reach the Bay of Los Angeles, but there was the horren-
dous road for which Baja was famous, and which carried the sign-
posts of dead vehicles along the roadway, like rusting corpses of a
military operation gone sour. If the boat was too heavy, the road,

which was really little more than river bed, would, in all probability cause an axle to break or a U-bolt to snap, which is precisely what occurred in '67, aborting one of the two campaigns to Guardian Angel in that year.

The other expedition was successful and returned with the sort of tales that, in those early days of underwater hunting, on a breath-hold dive, against the biggest, strongest, and toughest fish in the world, the Gulf grouper, was enough to encourage even the faintest of heart to pursue the unimaginable, and arrange a foray into those wild and unpredictable waters.

The logical choice in that spring of '68 was to launch out of San Felipe and run ninety miles along inhospitable and desolate coastline hoping to find fuel on the way, and take our chances with the Gulf winds that can turn placid waters into roaring seas in a matter of moments.

Frank Taylor had been on that '67 trip, and now, on an utterly clear and windless spring morning, with the sun breaking over the water, (a rare sight for a Californian), Frank, Bill Brown and myself settled into Frank's twenty-one-foot open boat, the Osprey, and atop glassy seas, skated our way under a relentless sun to Puertecitos. The first leg of our trip was deliriously smooth and without incident. Without much trouble, we found fuel in Puertecitos, filtered it through a tee shirt as the infamous tide of the Gulf ran out, nearly leaving us high and dry, and continued south, paralleling the coast-line.

Near the scattered islands of the Mid-riff, that rose stark and volcanic out of the azure sea, the afternoon winds rose out of the east and plunged us into gathering seas. Under half throttle we made the Gonzaga inlet before dusk, and camped at Papa Fernandez settle-ment which was little more than a cluster of shacks built of tar paper, and corrugated tin sheets. That night we lifted a few beers in the Cardboard Cantina, and in the course of the high spirited evening we let our destination be known. The locals grinned gap-toothed grins at each other, as if to say, the Gulf will have these gringos for breakfast.

In the morning with no fuel to spare at Papa Fernandez, we went across the bay to Alfonsina's. They too were without fuel, but passed on a rumor of a hermit who was hoarding fifty gallons in a deserted fishing camp on the other side of the Bay. "Be careful," we were warned, "he has a gun."

We found the abandoned fishing village and the hermit, who had waited perhaps years for this occasion, and without the need of a gun holds us up for the fuel. We were baffled by how the fuel could have found its way to this God-forsaken camp, and by what means the hermit came by it. Flakes of rust, like iron dandruff, gathered in the bottom of the fuel buckets. We must hiked down to the boat and then filter the fuel with tee shirts, which we doubled up to protect against serious contamination. The very last thing we needed was engine problems. For on the Gulf you were strictly on your own, no Coast Guard, no radio contact, no auxiliary boat patrol; nothing but your small boat in a channel where winds can rise to ninety miles an hour from almost any direction at any time, making it one of the more volatile bodies of water in the hemisphere.

By the time we had carried the fuel down to the boat and filtered it, the sun had reached its zenith and was beginning to fall. The wind had picked up, and a chop was building. We pressed on out into open water, bucking quartering swells that now came out of the south.

Five minutes off shore we began to take a pounding, and put on our wet suits and face masks so we could see through the sea spray that was exploding over the bow. In an hour we had scarcely traveled five miles.

It was not for petty considerations that so few had reached the island. In those long moments I understood why the island had never seen a spearfisherman, save for those in '67. It appeared that we were on the Sea of Hades, heading straight for disaster, and I was growing more anxious by the moment. Guardian Angel loomed like a grand monolith of an island, (the largest island in the Gulf) beckoning us ever onward, and in the crystalline air seemed closer than it actually was. The seas grew worse. I had never experienced such water and could only imagine what might await us in the middle of this raging strait. Frank was a Commander in the Navy, a graduate of Annapolis who had once skippered a destroyer off Viet Nam. He unquestionably knew his stuff, and as the Osprey twisted and torqued, and sea spray engulfed the boat, he turned to me and asked my assessment of the situation. To which I replied unhesitatingly, "let's turn back."

To my utter amazement, he did. Later, on other excursions to other parts of the world, I learned there is a certain wisdom in allocating validity to a coward's plea, for often the coward can see what the brave are blind to.

We returned to the hermit's beach and camped there for the

night. At daybreak the next morning the winds had died and we shoved off to a bright and glorious morning, riding a fair sea across the Gulf. Some ten miles from the north end of the island, Sail Rock stood as a white-triangled mainsail from a great schooner of the past. When we were upon it, the rock itself was a majestic pinnacle of sculpture and bird dung standing sixty feet high in cobalt blue water that fortified the spearfishing fantasy and set the blood to running with anticipation.

For all the underwater fantasies yet to be fulfilled, there was before us the stunning power and isolated imminence of Guardian Angel itself. Sea birds of every description wheeled in the cornflower sky; terns, gulls, pelicans, (of which we later found nesting grounds on the high cliffs), cormorant, and osprey flooded the heavens on winged patrols. On the extreme north end of the island there were islands within bays that opposed the other as to give the illusion that sanctuary for boat or bird, beast or man, was boundless, and no doubt the source of the island's namesake. A half mile square island in the middle of a bay housed a colony of sea lions that numbered well over five hundred. There were grand formations of rock and weathered portals in stone that dwarfed the human figure. Never in my days of travel, before or since, had I been witness to such a display of natural grandeur that so suggested the element of pristine magic. It was due, no doubt, to its isolated status from man, in what was, at that time, as wild a section of the world as the jungles of the upper Amazon or some other wilderness in its days before the arrival of civilized man. We were bewitched and had not yet made a dive.

We anchored on a spot that was obvious grouper territory, directly over a rock outcropping and reef, eighty feet to sand.

The underwater visibility was clearer than was typical of the Gulf, which generally is hazy due in large part to the overwhelming richness of sea life. And in this regard, Guardian Angel was no different, for schools of minute fish clouded the otherwise fifty-foot visibility. On my first dive I passed through a cloud of fish only to encounter another beneath it, and so it went clear to the seventy-foot bottom, where great black shapes of grouper drifted as small sunken ships aroused from their sea graves.

While I had not seen many grouper in two previous trips to the Gulf, these were far and away the largest I had ever encountered, ranging between sixty and a hundred pounds, and upon my approach, slid off down to the bottom and then turned to observe the clumsy intruder. The first sighting left me breathless and I ascended quickly. Over the course of the next half a dozen dives, I came across a leatherback turtle, that, to this day, was the largest I had ever seen. I located, in casual passing, a cave chock full of lobsters, all eight to ten pounds. I speared my first grouper near a hundred pounds, and had my first serious shark encounter. It was quite a morning.

We had determined that each diver would only take one fish a day, for that was the limit of our ice and chests. Frank speared his fish in short order, and Bill, never much of a hunter, abandoned his speargun for a camera. With the spearfishing done for the day, Frank had a very special surprise. The '67 group, who had endured wind and current their first day on the island, had sought sanctuary in a rather nondescript cove where they anchored to wait out the rough weather. A small reef hugged the shore, and one diver thought that it might hold lobster so went in to scout it. He found instead an extensive reef that descended to a fifty-foot-bottom, and was inhabited by grouper, score upon score of them, all eighty to a hundred pounders. A spearfisherman's dream of the sort Guardian Angel would become renowned for in the years to come. Quite naturally this news should have been met with a great deal of enthusiasm borne from the labors of their journey. However, upon learning what lay beneath them, the '67 group made a remarkably uncharacteristic and heroic pact; they elected not to hunt the fish. One must keep in mind that this was before the days of an environmental conscious-ness, and to resist the temptation that would not have significantly impacted the population was indeed noble. More, it was a declaration of their deep respect and understanding of the ocean creatures that they hunted, and for which no others outside of the hunting experi-ence could truly comprehend. (I must also remind that I am speaking of one-to-one hunting, a very personal undertaking, not the wanton killing of fish by use of nets or other such impersonal devices.) So there it was, a reef that the tribe had chosen to honor and keep intact as it might have been for a thousand years. We could do no less than to honor and uphold their commitment of preservation.

I dropped down to thirty feet and settled on a boulder and waited. From every direction came black behemoths of underwater majesty and power. Curious, fearless, their pectoral fins, like dinner plates fanning the water, bringing them as close as four feet away. From that distance we would gaze in rapt curiosity at one another until I was out of air and had to ascend to the surface. To be in the same water with such powerful creatures that had such obvious command of their element is like no other experience. In those moments something magical occurs and the sacredness of an untouched wilderness takes on new meaning.

Dive after dive the same pattern would unfold. I would lay on the rock and the grouper would come and inspect. I moved about the reef, and encountered different fish all very much as interested in me as I in them. The experience was deeply profound and I dove until exhaustion. That night, around the camp fire we christened the reef, "The Aquarium." More than a place in the sea, it was a place in all of us that longed to keep intact the magic of a rich wilderness. We understood what it meant to preserve something precious that transcended our own selfish occupation of the planet.

Fast forward ten years to 1978.

I had been fortunate enough to have spent a great deal of time in the Gulf during that decade. And had managed to visit Guardian Angel and the Aquarium on ive different occasions, and knew of no one who had been so privileged. For that reason I had been asked to act as a spearfishing guide and accompany a party of hunters back into the Mid-riff in the fall of 1978.

This time down there would be no rough roads for me, no campouts in the dirt along the highway, no broken axles, nor dented oil pans, nor snapped U-bolts, not even a worry of rough water, and best of all, no expenses. I was going first class. We were motoring down from San Felipe on an eighty-five-foot converted shrimp trawler. Aboard were pangas, (fourteen foot Mexican skiffs that would be launched when the mother ship anchored), that permitted the hunters to work from boats that were quick and had easy access in and out of the water. With three hot meals a day, cold beers, and unlimited ice in the hold for fish, it was the antithesis of those early days in the Gulf, and I adapted with remarkable ease.

Yet for all those conveniences one still had to get into the water and find the big fish. That was my job, more or less, to locate the big fish. It should have been easy, but we ran into a plankton bloom that turned the water a rust color and reduced underwater visibility to about a foot. In addition, strong currents were pushing the fish down in those areas we found decent visibility. We pushed through Salvaterria, and the high Mid-riff islands down to the north end of Guardian Angel where the conditions had not improved. We worked our way down the island all the way to the southern tip and then beyond to the islands below, and while the visibility had improved somewhat, the hunting was poor and no big fish were taken. The eight days dragged fruitlessly by, and we turned for the long run back to San Felipe.

I don't know whether it was because I felt an obligation to produce the fish I had promised, or if my ego as "the big game spearfishing guide," claimed my judgment, but I gathered my two principals aside and told them about the Aquarium. I explained that it had remained a preserve within the tribe of hunters for as long as we had known about it. If they would promise to take one fish each, I would disclose its location.

They readily agreed.

We arrived back on the north end and instructed the captain to anchor in a cove that was out of view and around the corner from the Aquarium. A panga was lowered and the two divers, myself and the Mexican boatman swung around and out of sight of the trawler and headed for the reef. The reef was as inhabited as it had always been, and the hunters were appropriately overwhelmed. Within minutes they each landed a fish near a hundred pounds. They were quite naturally grateful and solemnly declared that the secret was safe with them and that they would never again violate those waters. I felt a debt to them had been paid, though to a degree I also felt that I had betrayed members of the tribe who had endeavored to preserve the reef. I rationalized the decision by telling myself it was only two fish out of perhaps a hundred or more, and in the grand scheme of things, they would scarcely be missed. Under the circumstances I felt I could live with my indiscretion.

The following year I was again the guide for the same group on a similar boat down to the same islands. That year the water was clear, the currents mild, and the hunting was good. After a successful week we decided to check out the Aquarium on the trip back up Guardian Angel, for no other reason than to witness the grand spectacle of the grouper at play in their sanctuary. For as many times as I had seen it, it was always a thrill, and the two other divers were looking forward to it as well.

As soon as I dropped into the water I knew something was very wrong. Inhaling a breath into a tight stomach that was sensing something ominous in the water, I dove cautiously. There was scarcely a sign of fish. The bait fish, and cabrillo that usually filled every seam in the reef were absent, and there was no sign of the grouper. Up for air and down again, deeper this time, I settled on a boulder and waited for the length of a breath-hold; nothing. Empty as a graveyard save for the stark boulders that resembled tombstones in the sand.

We covered the entire reef, and didn't find a single fish. It was inexplicable. I was utterly dismayed. Why would fish suddenly abandon a place that had been home for the last ten years, and perhaps a hundred before that? I was at a loss for an explanation. We, like burdened pallbearers, returned to the mother ship, weighed anchor and began that last long leg for San Felipe. I laid in my bunk for most of the trip trying to figure out what had happened. Then, just before falling asleep the night we were due to arrive, it came to me, as an electric shock that immediately deadens the senses; I had forgotten about the Mexican boatman who was operating the panga.

Like the Judas goat who leads the lambs to slaughter, and is thus spared its life to lead the next flock to its eventual death, I had led the Mexicans to the reef and they, over a period of a year, had methodically fished every grouper off the reef, until there were none. Unlike the Judas goat who knows no guilt in its betrayal of his brethren, I now had to live with the realization that I was responsible. I had played a role in the ever diminishing abundance of wildlife that once ran wild and free in the waters of the planet. And unlike the gill netter, or the purse seiner, or the long liner, and all who have taken so greedily from the belly of the mother, I have seen the barren space that is left, and forever will carry the weight of that emptiness in my heart.

c. e.
summer of '91

The One I Wished Had Got Away

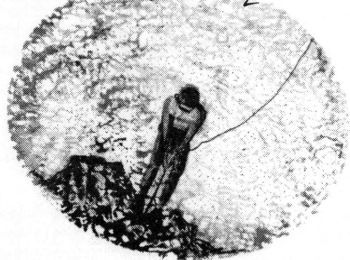

THERE IS ALWAYS TALK among spearfishermen, as well as fishermen, and I suppose among hunters of every kind on every continent, about the ones that got away. I've had my share, though two seem to stand out among the rest. One fish, a grouper, really never got away in the sense that I tried to spear it. Further explanation, if I might digress for a moment, appears necessary.

I was down on a trip to Guardian Angel island which lays monolithically in the northern waters of the Sea of Cortez, in what is called the Mid-riff. We launched out of the Bay of Los Angeles after a twelve-hour drive over the newly paved road from the border at Tijuana. From there it was a three hour jump over rather precarious waters to the island. We had clear sailing, and reached the north end of the island without incident. (Such a trip would have been considered an absolute lark just two years prior, before the road was built.) In that time span we leaped from industrialized civilization at its worst into a virtually untouched wilderness that rivaled the savannas of East Africa in its pre-settlement years. We reached the island without incident, and before entering the water for the first time, we reaffirmed our guidelines for hunting fish in the Gulf, (as the Sea of Cortez was commonly called). There was but one hard and fast rule; no more than one fish a day per person would be taken. We carried back our meat and there were only two ice chests a man. When they were full, the hunting was done. It came down to one fish a day, period, no exceptions.

Early the second morning I had speared my fish, and including the one yesterday, had already filled both ice chests. Though there were two days to go, I was finished for the trip. It had been loosely agreed that the first hunter who landed his fish would do the dinner hunt in the afternoon for a fish of no more than fifteen pounds. So in the late afternoon we dropped anchor near a severe drop off, and I went over the side. As I cocked my speargun, a grouper the size of which I could not begin to calculate, came up from the depths to investigate the noise of the anchor that had clanged on the rocks in thirty feet of water. The fish hovered over the anchor, while I, still on the surface and directly behind it, prepared to dive. It was the largest grouper I had ever seen, or will ever expect to see anytime, anywhere. It's difficult to judge weight of really large fish. I had been in the water with fish that were over four hundred pounds, so I was not without a yardstick. (I believe the record for grouper in the Gulf at that time might have been around a hundred and twenty-five pounds. It was a rare occurrence when anyone pulled out a grouper of over a hundred pounds.) At any rate I judged this fish to be well over two hundred pounds. A world record if ever there was one. I was right on top of it. It never saw me as I dropped down and leveled the gun behind its pectoral fin. I hung there wondering how many ice chests I would have had to bring to permit me to spear this fish. I imagined the spear shaft hitting the grouper and the tremendous fight that would ensue. And the indescribable feeling that comes when a powerful fish is at the other end of the line, its strength pitted against my own strength. A supreme struggle that always thrusts me back into another time that is simple, pure, primitive and eternal. An incredibly exhilarating moment that is wholly unpredictable in its outcome. The fish eventually caught my movement, eyed me disdainfully and then slid to the depths from where it had come, disappearing into the inky blue.

Fish and records come and go. Names are scribbled into record books, perhaps forever immortalizing the hunter. I, on occasion, look back on that moment, but never with regret. For there is another book far more important. One that registers every act that we commit, it is held in our stomachs and chests, we carry it in our walk, and the way our eyes meet another's. The book is us, and we must read it everyday.

I trust I haven't given the impression of a virtuousness that I don't possess. It is not my intention to imply that I regularly make a habit of rejecting opportunities to land record fish. Quite the contrary, I, if I am nothing else, am a hunter. And there was a time in my life when I would gladly have given a body part to land a world record white sea bass. I clearly had my chance.

White sea bass are not just any fish. They don't have the overwhelming power and toughness of the gulf grouper or pargo that demands a deep dive and the breath-hold of Neptune to endure the initial charge that can drag a man across boulder and reef, to the depths. Nor do they display the run of the amberjack, rooster, wahoo, or tuna that can tow a boat, much less a man, some distance in open water. No, the white sea bass is a refined fish of grand sophistication. It survives on cunning, stealth, and a hypersensitivity to its surroundings, and will remove itself from the vicinity of any disturbance, however slight it might be. Its territory is not the open water, but the kelp forests, where it slides silently, ghost-like among the kelp trees, an apparition in colors of the sea.

As I have described in detail in the book, *The Last of the Blue Water Hunters*, to track the white sea bass one must think like a white sea bass, move like a white sea bass and become as hypersensitive to the underwater environment as a white sea bass. One must be willing to patiently track them in the endless forests at the first light of day and into the last light of dusk. In the interim one must study their habits, and in the doing will extract more from the sea's infinite knowledge than any book or man could possibly convey.

Having said that, and having spent decades in search for the white sea bass, you may rest assured that at one time, I did indeed covet the world record. Which, it seemed was always just out of my grasp, when I landed a sixty-six pounder the record was seventy-one, and when I landed a seventy-two pounder it was where it has been for the last fifteen years, and apparently where it will remain, (or so it would seem based on the size of fish being speared this last decade and a half), in the capable hands of one of the finest hunters of fish I have ever known, the late Yas Ikeda, at the weight of seventy seven pounds. I had always figured that if I spent enough time in the water my chance to break Yas's record would come. One day it did.

We were diving off Church Rock, which in the seventies was the hot spot for whites, and had anchored outside the rock some distance because a big swell was running. It didn't look good. The kelp was down and the water appeared to be tinged with green, but one can never truly judge visibility from the deck of a boat. So I went in to check it out, and swam in from deep water towards the line of kelp that was strung on a reef that rested as a long pew in front of Church Rock and was usually the place we picked up fish. At the kelp line there was a surface haze for the first fifteen feet and then it opened up nicely to fifty feet, however a strong current was running and the kelp was laying down; unsuitable conditions for hunting white sea bass, and so I headed back to the boat.

Halfway, I came across a single strand of kelp, one I had never seen. It was way out in the middle of nowhere, and without taking much of a breath I just instinctively dove on it, for no other reason than I had not come across it before. Such is the nature of hunters and the attraction to the undertaking. For perhaps this one spot might yield an undiscovered reef that would be a congregation point for who knows what, whites, yellows, blacks, tuna; the possibilities were endless in those glory days. I dropped beneath the surface haze and, in very deep water, near the sand there glimmered a flicker of light. I continued to drop, driven by curiosity, and at sixty feet there materialized on the sand at eighty feet, a white sea bass that was of a size that defied belief. A conservative guess put the fish at a hundred and twenty pounds, easily a world record. The instant I saw the fish I knew it was a world record, one that would never be broken. I was dropping like a rock, and had only seconds to make a series of decisions. In addition I had not taken a full breath and was already at the end of my breath-hold and began to think how this fish, which was longer than me and as big around as an IRS file cabinet, was going to give one hell of a ride. Such thoughts doom a stalk. One cannot afford to think when stalking a fish. In fact, to be a successful spearfisherman, one must avoid all thought and simply react to the situation. But I was thinking and falling, and had only seconds to get off a decent shot. The fish had sensed me and was beginning to move. I might have taken a shot right then, from the top, straight down. It would have been a difficult shot but its back was plenty wide and in retrospect was probably the best available shot. But I was thinking, and passed it up to level off parallel with the fish and try for a broadside. The fish had seen me as I leveled out for the shot. (It was so big that it was unable to sprint away in a flash as smaller fish do.) The whole body had to move in order to generate the enormous tail into motion. The effect was similar to the motion of a snake moving through grass. I lined up quickly, had a wide open shot as the fish was swinging back and forth putting distance between us, and pulled the trigger. The shaft ran straight along the side of the fish, where it had just been, past its head, and then in slow motion, fell harmlessly in the sand. I was stunned. The record had been handed to me and I had managed to blow it. I knew in that moment I would never have another opportunity. The white sea bass vanished out to sea as I kicked for the surface.

It was a long way up.

I have digressed much further than intended. After all, the title of this piece is not, "The Ones that Got Away," but, "The One I Wish Had Got Away." Perhaps more accurately, "The One I Wish I Had Never Speared." An odd title perhaps, but certainly in keeping with that old axiom, 'Be careful what you wish for because one day you shall have it.'

Onward.

By the early eighties, ten years after the Baja road had been connected, I had spent a great deal of time spearing fish down in the Gulf. I was not without my successes, and had become quite confident, if not cocky in my perceived abilities to land just about any fish that swam in those waters. Having grown weary of using a dragline that trailed a hundred feet behind the gun and almost insured a fish if the placement of the spear was decent, I decided that the insurance of a dragline was for those careless in their spear placement and soft of leg and lung. I would spear fish with just a shooting line, and then horse it up off the bottom on leg strength, and breath-hold power. I rigged one of my guns with some beefy cable for shooting line, and that was it, no dragline, no reel.

A week later, on a blazing fall morning, I and two fellow hunters launched my fourteen-foot skiff, the Low Now, out of the Bay of Los Angeles with intentions of camping eight to twelve miles south of the Bay and hunt in waters that were still relatively untouched.

This we did, and in the afternoon after setting up camp, we were on the water looking for game. I, with my re-rigged speargun, brimming with confidence only the truly disillusioned possess, dropped down on a grouper in a boulder-strewn bottom and put a shaft in what appeared to be a fish of about sixty pounds. It powered off down a ledge, and though kicking furiously, I was unable to halt its run in any appreciable way. It, as groupers commonly do, found a cave and darted into it. In the short time my breath-hold permitted I attempted, unsuccessfully, to pull the fish from the cave. Then, leaving the speargun floating above the cave, I ascended to the surface for a breath. The cave was not deep, maybe fifty feet. Once I re-fueled my lungs it would simply be a matter of *diving* down, *reaching* into the cave, closing fish's gills, (which grouper and other reef fish open up to wedge themselves tight into a cave), and pulling the fish out. No problem.

Upon arriving at the cave, I discovered that it was too small for me to squeeze my shoulders through and too deep to extend my arms and get a hold of the fish. No problem. I'll just put both feet against either side of the cave for leverage and using leg and arm strength pull the fish out with brute force. I'd done it many a time with scarcely a failure.

Evidently this fish didn't know who it was dealing with, because I couldn't budge it. After making a dozen dives, I was no closer to extracting the grouper than when I had started. The two divers had gathered in the skiff and were having a marvelous time with my misfortune, offering me their draglines and spears should I wish to join their cadre of good sense. As if to punctuate my folly, there appeared a large, dusky shark that was beginning to twist on the blood spoor that was seeping from the cave.

No problem. I'll assume humility and use my other gun, the one with the dragline, to spear the fish again, and tie the end of the line to the boat and pull it out of the cave on the force of twenty-five horses.

This I did, after dodging the dusky and aiming a somewhat blind shot into the cave, directed only by the spear-point cable in the approximate location of the fish. I brought up the dragline and we tied it to the stern of the boat and cranked up the rpm's. Nothing. All I did was bend the spear shaft into a U-shape and attract two more sharks.

The sun had dropped behind the mountain range in the west and the sky showed a tint of orange. The situation was quickly losing its funny bone. We had to get that fish out before we lost light, and before there were too many more sharks to make working conditions less than hospitable. I tried again, cranking hard on the outboard, nothing. I backed it down to get a better angle, when the engine stopped. The prop had caught the dragline and wrapped it. The entire lower unit looked like a yellow beach ball. The line was so tight we couldn't tilt the engine out of the water.

Up to this point it had become a circus and I was the ringmaster, but now we had some hard decisions to make. The choices were few. We would have to cut the line off the prop, and either cut the cable off the shooting line of the other gun, and leave the fish, or tie a line to the floating gun and buoy the rig and come back for it tomorrow morning. Alas, consistent with my dull-witted deeds, I had neglected to bring cable cutters, so the first alternative was out. In addition, I did not want to cut the fish loose. There was an unwritten law that all spearfishermen strictly adhere to. One does not abandon a speared fish, every effort must be made to bring a fish to the boat. No, we would not cut the fish loose. We couldn't, even if we wanted to, Carlos forgot the cable cutters. Okay, we buoy the gun. No, bad idea. Oftentimes a speared fish will abandon its refuge in the dead of night and swim off to parts unknown either to recover from its wound or to die. In the doing it, would take the gun with it and most certainly we'd be unable to find it in the morning. There was also the possibility that a fisherman might come along and lift the buoy; all is fair in open water. If the fish was loose he could claim it as his own along with the gun; if not, he might just cut the buoy from the line if he happens to need a buoy, and we might never relocate the fish.

After having eliminated the logical possibilities, I began to ponder schemes that, I'm sure to my companions at least, were now crossing over the line into the moronic. (Apparently, I was more comfortable playing in that ball park.) As the last vestiges of blue slipped from the sky, and as the sharks continued to gather, (reducing the volunteers to none who would be willing to dangle in the night water for a half an hour while trying to cut the line off the prop), I suggested we anchor the boat off the bow, and swim ashore. One man stays in the boat for the night, and in the morning we pick up where we left off.

Everyone agreed. It sounded like a good plan.

Who was going to spend the night in the boat without dinner, laying cold under a wet wet suit, with only a jug of water to keep him company? Not surprising, there were no volunteers.

"Shall we draw lots?" I suggested.

No?

Carlos' fish, his gun, his boat, his dilemma. Guess who'll stay?

No problem. But there was a problem, a big problem. I didn't want to stay in that smelly boat all night, cold and wet with nothing to eat. I was not nearly so tough as I pretended to be. I wanted a hot meal and a good sleep around the fire. The shoreline was a half mile away and we could walk back to camp several miles, then return in the morning just as the sun came up before any fishermen would come across the boat and claim it for their own. It was of course a terrible idea, one born of desperation and weak character, but it seemed to be the thing to do at the time.

Leaving the boat anchored firmly in the bow, and not completely ignorant of the potential for disaster, I managed to unwrap a couple of top loops from around the prop and fasten the line to the boat; so we wouldn't return and find the lower unit of the outboard resting on the bottom of the ocean.

We entered the water with a half dozen sharks milling around barely visible beneath the boat, and swam ashore less than leisurely.

Night fell like the shadow of a great white shark, and we stumbled ashore and began walking along the cruel shoreline, stubbing toes and falling over every rock and boulder that Baja could offer on such short notice. We reached camp exhausted. The wind began to come up as we finished dinner, and I visualized the Low Now being swept out into the Gulf, and my two thousand dollar outfit winding up in Mazatlan, the pride of a ne'er-do-well fisherman. I couldn't sleep, and at three in the morning awoke my comrades with a plan. One would go out on the far point and try to hail any passing boats. One would stay in camp and keep a fire going. And I would make the torturous walk back to the beach we came in on and swim out to the boat. If in two hours I had not returned, the keeper of the fire would set out to join me.

My musings were as dark as the dawn. Why did I ever leave the boat? Such stupidity could only result in yet another catastrophe. Why did I spear a fish without a dragline, why, why, why? I came to the place were we had left the water the night before and sat on a high spot awaiting the sun. I could not yet see the boat. The sun broke the horizon like a neon orange that spilled its electric juice into the sea. And still I couldn't locate the boat. It was nowhere in sight. Such a loss at this point was almost expected. Then, out toward the far horizon across the slick sea of orange juice, rested the Low Now. It was maybe a four mile swim, maybe more. In the clear Baja air, it was either an illusion of being very far away, or it actually was very far away. It didn't matter; I was determined to retrieve my boat. I took bearings off the sun and headed into the water with wet suit, mask, fins and snorkel, leaving my weight belt on the beach.

As the bottom dropped away to open water, I lost the illusion of comfort and began to think; which is what I should have done before

I entered the water. Several hundred yards offshore I was beginning to have those familiar feelings of naked vulnerability. What would it be like two miles from the shoreline, three miles? I should have brought a gun.

I kept swimming.

I was swimming strong and steady and had taken bearings off the sun, and then calculated the angle of the rays as they penetrated the water. If I maintained that angle I wouldn't have to look up every minute for a sun bearing. Though, on occasion I did glance back to shore to measure my swim, and get a bearing off points of land to confirm my heading. I figured if a current was running, and in all likelihood one was, I would just keep swimming off my bearings. The current would be moving the skiff and me with the same speed. It occurred to me that if the wind came up, I would be having different and far more severe problems. The wind would push the boat, and the ruffled seas would make for a difficult sighting. I prayed for no wind.

When a young man who has lived in and around the sea all his life and is of strong leg and lung, and does not respect the sea as perhaps he should, begins to experience severe fatigue, the like of which numbs the body, his fear rises like an ice phantom out of the glacier of his denial and begins to whisper of frailties and weakness. It is then that the water becomes infinite, and less distinct. And images form in darkened nondescript shapes, boiling just beyond sharp visibility. He will suddenly turn to counter the approach of a demon that he is certain is behind him. And his kicks seem to thrash in panic as if in calling Eumenides from the depths to avenge his every misdeed in the sea.

Past the point of no return.

I stopped and attempted to locate the boat. A light breeze was stirring the water; I couldn't find it. Looking back to shore which seemed to be near, yet was very far, I suddenly became aware that the current had pushed me far south. Unable to find the skiff fueled my suppressed anxiety that wanted to ignite into panic. My legs drained of strength, my belly tightened, and my throat constricted. Oddly, it was in this state that I realized with acute clarity that if the wind were to increase and I couldn't find the boat, I'd be unable to make the swim back. I had gone too far already, and the current was pushing me farther and farther off shore. Also, if a fisherman were to happen by he would be unable to see me in a rolling sea. The full impact of my predicament rendered me torpid. With great effort I attempted to get my legs moving again. I must find the boat, and I must find it soon. There was nothing else to think about, nothing else to do, but find the boat. My body unwound a bit and I started to swim. I couldn't make my legs new and strong again; but I could make my mind strong. I focused down on the swim and obliterated everything from my mind. As soon as something negative entered, like sharks, or failure, I immediately dismissed it and continued to swim.

The sun was very high now and the angle of the rays through the water had changed. I was unsure of my bearings. I didn't even bother to look back to shore. It was like looking out of the window of a skyscraper to the street below. The skiff was still out there, some-where bobbing and waiting. Maybe it's not out there at all. Maybe some fisherman has found it and has taken it to Mazatlan. I am chasing a mirage, an apparition; I am chasing myself right into oblivion.

I put my face back into the water and resumed swimming.

I wonder if they will ever find me; if my body will someday wash up on a beach? Which beach? Who will find it? No one will find it. The sharks will have me for dinner. By nightfall I'll be fodder for the Gulf sharks.

I kept swimming, but I don't know how, or even why.

At some point I realized that I was not swimming. I only thought I was swimming. My legs were not moving. They had nowhere to go. No destination. No home. No place to rest. My legs had given up and they didn't even tell me.

The wind was rising. I was not far behind my legs.

I looked out across the Gulf, not even sure what I was looking for, not sure what the skiff looked like anymore. It wasn't there. I made a slow three-sixty-turn, and there it was, not a hundred yards away. Not out to sea, but north, the last place I would have thought it to be. Had I swum past it, going south. Had I swum another five minutes I would have missed it entirely, with no chance of seeing it again.

I dog-paddled over to the boat. Beneath her, the one spear shaft dangled bent like pretzeled rebar, the cabled point hanging in the wind of the current. The other speargun, the one I had rigged with-out the dragline, the one that very nearly punched my ticket, was gone, and I felt no loss. I might have thrown it away myself if it was still somehow attached, but the sea had done that for me, and I was obliged. Naturally there was no sign of the fish, no sign of anything. The bow anchor was hanging straight down into the infinite blue, waiting for shallow water to re-employ it. I could scarcely crawl into the boat, but once in, the feeling of something solid, like life reborn, was heavenly. I drank water and stared at the sky for a very long time.

I figured the fish must have decided to make a run for it and the sharks got it, pulling the anchor loose. Maybe it was the wind, maybe both. Another ocean mystery among millions. I still had to cut the line loose from the prop. But I was in no hurry, I had plenty of time now, plenty of time.

c. e.
summer of '91

The Bay

I T WASN'T THAT MANY YEARS AGO when Mom and I would sit on the big boulder in front of the bay while Dad got into his wet suit and then went off into the water. We'd watch him from there and count the seconds of his dives. I learned to count up to a hundred and twenty on that boulder. Sometimes the tide would come in and turn our sitting place into an island, and we'd have to wait until Dad came back so he could carry us to high ground. After every dive he'd let me peek inside the bag that hung beneath the inner tube. It was always filled with amazing things. Different kinds of fish, or lobster, or abalone. There was always plenty of abalone in those days. I liked to watch them crawl around in there looking to stick to something.

It seemed like I grew up on that boulder. Next to being in the water when I was older, being on that boulder with Dad was like being with a magician who was showing you how he did his tricks.

He'd been diving that bay long before I was born, long before there was a house on the highway, and he'd have to cut across open land for a quarter mile just to reach the water.

Anyway, we'd sit on that big old boulder and look out across the mirror surface of the water that was unknown and secret, and he'd turn it transparent before my eyes.

Pointing to some vacant area of surface water he'd say, "Right over there is a long reef that juts directly out to sea. It's got a pocket of old lobsters there that I've been picking for fifteen years. Three big sheepshead are on that reef and every so often I'll throw them a lobster. Sheepshead love lobster. There's one I call 'Beef' because he's bright red and as big as a side of beef. Old Beef and I got to know each other pretty good over the years and it got to where he'd lead me to lobster holes and then wait for me to give him one. I'd bring it out into the open and let it go, and he'd be on it in a flash, and take the whole thing in his mouth, nothing but two antenna sticking out of those lips as he swam off." Dad would laugh and shake his head at this incredible sight only he had seen.

There must have been twenty or so reefs in the bay and he'd have a story or two for each one. In between stories he'd gaze out on the water, his face all crinkled and full of knowledge, looking like the ocean floor itself. He'd get all quiet and peaceful, and I knew he was down there again, feeling the sea all around him, holding his breath, seeing worlds that I could only imagine.

Dad's job was machining metal, but his love was the sea. There was times when he got laid off, and it would bother Mom something terrible; she was always worried where the money was going to come from. But Dad would just say, "We got the bay, we don't need no money." And he was right, our family ate abalone and scallops the way most families eat potatoes. He always took exactly what we needed; no more, no less. "Every man should have to hunt for his food," he once said. "It not only gives him a sense of the natural balance of things, but he would never again take the death of a creature lightly, or eat his meals without giving some thanks for what was before him."

I used to wonder out loud, "How many folks you suppose believe that fish are swimming along wrapped in that plastic they cover them with in the store?"

The first time I said that, Dad laughed so hard I thought he was going to bust a gut.

In the summer of my seventh year, he took me over the rocks to the south end of the bay where there was another sort of rocky cove that was off by itself. There were big tide pools in this cove, and they sat gleaming in the sun like slabs of new ice.

"These tide pools are like a slice of the bigger ocean," Dad told me. "They look the same as the bay, except smaller, but you got to treat them as if you were under the water. And that means coming up to them slow and careful, keep the sun to your face so you won't cast a shadow and spook the critters. They're just the same as ocean critters; they all spook to movement."

We snuck up on this one pool and he whispered, "You won't see nothing right away, but if you stay quiet, and not look too hard, sort of gaze, you can begin to spot them. Its the same way under the water. Always go slow and easy and let the ocean come into your eyes instead of you reaching out for it. You see more that way."

Pretty soon the tide pool began to stir with life. Where before there was weed and stone, now there was hermit crabs in shell houses scrambling around each other. Tiny fish appeared near the flowering sea anemone and a starfish leg grew out from under a ledge. Dad showed me an octopus that looked more like a brown stone until it moved. In the diamond waters it seemed the tide pool was just oozing with life.

"Make yourself small," whispered Dad. "Take your imagination into the pool and pretend to swim along its drop-offs and feel your way into its hidden places. That's where the real discoveries are."

I did, and became lost in the secrets of those pools. That first day we stayed until dusk, and watched the sun turn the sea to blood.

"Can you smell the change?" asked Dad. "The sea of day smells different from the night sea; stronger, can make a man drunk with it. Just like a woman. Be careful of night oceans and night women," he laughed. "Both are dangerous."

After winter storms Dad would take me walking down the beach, which was over a mile long. He'd kick over piles of kelp and seaweed as we went along, looking for a sign. "Look, a big lobster carcass. The old boy molted it last fall. Well we know he's still out there don't we." He'd hand it to me and I'd turn it over in my hand, trying to imagine it as something alive.

"Green abalone," he'd say picking up a broken shell. Then he'd look out across the bay, his eye opening up the surface as if he could see the very crevice that particular abalone had come from.

When I got older, like around nine, he began talking to me different, and I knew he was getting ready to take me into the water with him. We'd sit on that boulder, and he'd tell me how things would change under the water with the seasons. "There's a strip of

sand that lies between the two distant outside reefs, near the blue
water. It jigs and jags like a wild river, and in the springtime the
halibut come in there to spawn. Who knows for how long they've
been doing that, maybe a thousand years, maybe more. But around
May and June there is always fifteen to thirty of them laying there in
that strip at one time. You just swim over them until you find the
right size that's going to take care of dinner for a couple of days."

That summer he gave me my first pair of fins and a mask and
snorkel, and baptized me, he called it, with the waters of the bay.
Mostly I held on to the inner tube, and looked on while he speared
fish. During that summer I learned where each reef lay, and he gave
me bearings to find them if I was to lose my way, which can happen
when you start diving, because everything looks pretty much the
same under the water. He showed me the lobster caves, and where to
find the abalone and scallops.

I kept a book on everything I saw and where I saw it. It was the
most magical summer of my entire life. And that's saying something
because every summer was filled with something new.

At the end of that summer; just before school was starting, me
and Dad was out on the boulder looking over the bay at sunset,
when he said real softly, "Now you know. Once you learn to dive,
you'll never go hungry. There'll be a temptation to start taking
everything you can lay your hands on, but you got to resist that
temptation. Only an ignorant person with no real understanding of
things would take for the sake of taking. If you just take what you
need, you'll always have plenty."

For the next two years Dad and I dove side by side, and he
passed on his knowledge to me. And I began to understand what he
meant by balance and harmony and how a man was a piece of the
picture rather than the artist who believed he drew it up.

Then in the spring of my thirteenth year, developers broke
ground for a bunch of houses, a planned community they called it,
across the highway, up from the bay. They were digging up the
ground to make a huge lake, and there was talk of a golf course.
Pretty soon all this mud and silt began to drain off into the bay,
turning it a sick, green color clear out to open water.

Dad and me couldn't dive it because the visibility shut down to nothing. He went to the developers and told them the bay was being fouled by the run-off, and they called the police and had him chased off the project. He went to the city and complained, and they said they'd look into the problem, but nothing was ever done.

"Everyone's getting rich from this development," declared Dad, "and they're stealing away the real wealth of this area, the beauty of the bay. They call it progress. Well maybe, but nobody seems to understand the price of their progress."

Mom would tell him not to take the whole thing so personal and that, "This is the way of our times. People are out to make money, and there's no stopping them. You're fighting a losing battle to try and save the bay."

Dad turned to me and asked quiet like, "And what do you think?"

Well I didn't like to see him get so worked up so I said, "I think Mom's right about this."

He shook his head real slow, and I knew that I gave him the wrong answer. "I figured you'd understood more than you do," he said. The words coming out tired and heavy from his chest. "I guess I wasn't the teacher I thought I was, or you wasn't the student I thought you were. To begin with, the bay can't speak for itself, at least not in the language of those interested in making a quick buck. The bay speaks to you and to me and to all of those who've ever enjoyed it. Joy is the thing that connects us to the things we love. There's nothing more natural than to care for something you love. That's how we became caretakers for the bay, sort of giving back to it all the good that it gave us. If we don't speak up for it, who will? Certainly not anyone who can't speak its language or hear its voice."

Course I knew he was right, and I was ashamed for not speaking my mind in the first place. I figured he understood, because he never reminded me of it again.

He fought a hard battle for the bay, but it was no use. After two years the digging and landscaping finally stopped; the lakes were filled and the golf course was green. Soon, folks were putting up fences with guards, and we had to walk way around just to get to the bay, but its waters were blue, and I could hardly wait to get in again.

We began to dive the bay together again, though alot of the fish had disappeared. Dad said it was because they couldn't see to feed. But the lobster and abalone and scallops were still around, and that summer I got my first ab and in the fall my first lobster. The diving seemed to revitalize Dad, who had aged considerably during those years out of the water, and he spoke about the bay's return to its old self.

"You know," he said one afternoon after a dive. "I don't have much to leave you after I die. My gift to you is this bay. I was afraid it'd be an empty and useless gift, but maybe I was a bit hasty. It feels good to fill our table again, and enjoy the gifts that are there for the asking. I hope that they'll be there for you long after I'm gone."

By the end of summer Dad began to notice that something was happening to the tide pools. "Come see," he said, "there's not a sea anemone in any of the pools. No sign of hermit crabs or fish. The vegetation seems to be dying away."

Sure enough the tide pools looked sick, like something was very wrong with them.

After our dives we'd go and see how they were doing, hoping they'd made a comeback, but little by little they gave up the life they so preciously held. By winter they were barren of life, and the remains hung on the craters like dead bile thrown up from the sea's sour belly. That's when the bay started showing signs of the same thing.

Then Dad got real sick, as though the bay and him had got some sort of terrible disease. Sometimes he was strong enough to go down to the beach and kick up the drift piles of kelp that was heaped up on the sand. "Look at this," he'd say like it was him that was personally hurt. "The color of the kelp is different; see how pale it is. It was dead before it hit the beach."

"Do you suppose its got something to do with the development?" I asked.

"That'd be the first place to look," he answered, looking up the hill to all those houses crowded together.

We went to the sales office and no one could tell us anything. A fellow in a shiny suit remembered Dad, "Your water is clean, what the hell are you complaining about now?"

"The water is dying," said Dad, "and there's no reason for it."

"Maybe it's just time for it to die," he laughed. "We all gotta go sometime."

"No, it don't work that way," explained Dad. "If it dies then we're not far behind it."

The shiny suit shook his head, still laughing, "Get outta here before I call the cops on you."

We went to city hall. And after being shuffled around from office to office, someone finally said the matter would be looked into. Dad was real tired and I had to help him to the car. "Am I the only one seeing what's going on?" He asked, kinda sad to himself. "Where are the others, the divers, and the surfers, and all the rest who've enjoyed a swim? Can't they see their bay is being killed in front of their eyes?"

"Maybe it'll get better," I said, trying to comfort him 'cuz I didn't want him to get any sicker. "The ocean is powerful, its been through millions of years of changes. I'm sure it can survive this."

"If you mean the physical water, yes, that will go on. From the surface all looks in good shape, but inside is the blood of the planet, the life force. Once you poison that, the rest will get weak and eventually can't fight anymore and give up and die."

When summer came, Dad was too sick to get out of bed. Mom looked worried all the time, and I didn't say anything but I was plenty worried too. One morning he called me to his bed. He was kind of out of his head. He told me to go down to the bay and have a look for myself. "See if them lobsters are in their caves, and if the fish are on the reefs."

In the morning I went down to the bay and put on my dive gear. I was pretty nervous because it was the first time I'd be diving alone. I wasn't scared, because I knew the bay, and there was nothing there that could hurt me. I was scared for reasons I couldn't quite figure out.

The water was as clear as I had ever seen it, and already I was feeling better. I figured with water this clean there should be plenty of sea life. The white sand reflected the high sun and the underwater brilliance lifted my hopes even further. The first reef that came into view was thirty yards from shore. It stood bare of kelp and seaweed in the white sand. I took a breath and dropped down for a look. There was an eerie feel to the place. It was as dead as a cemetery, and the scattered rocks reminded me of gravestones. The old roots of the kelp were bleached white, like bones of a skeleton. The sounds of the shrimp and undercurrent of noise that I always heard, was gone. The only sound was the beating of my heart.

I searched ten reefs. All the caves were empty of lobsters, and there was no sign of abalone. The rock scallops were stuck to their fate with their shells opened wide in a death gasp, and their insides rotted away to nothing, leaving it slick and white as a glass bowl.

Except for a single, pale fish, that lay in the sand, eyeing me in my rounds, I didn't see another living creature. I returned to the beach feeling empty and sick.

I sat on the boulder and looked out on the surface, and tried to imagine the bay back to life in my mind, the way it was as Dad had shown me when I was a kid, but it was useless. I sat there long into dusk asking, "How could this happen?"

Dad died within a week. I never told him about the bay, and he never asked, but I think he knew. He wanted me to spread his ashes across the waters of the bay. And when the time came, I begged Mom not to do it. I told her that we should wait until the bay got well again and be rich with sea life so it could hold Dad's soul like he wanted.

In the months that followed, half a dozen harbor seals washed up dead on the beach, and there was finally an investigation. Later it came out in the papers that the development had put something in their lakes that would keep them looking clean and pretty. When the spring rains came, the lakes overflowed and drained into the bay. And then after summer they emptied the lakes for cleaning, and thousands of gallons of this poison was run off into the bay.

It's been three years since they put an end to the pollution. The seaweed has come back to the reefs and the kelp beds are starting to show themselves again. I guess there are fish in the beds, though I haven't dove them. There hasn't been any sign of lobsters on the beach after the winter storms, and for that reason, I guess, I haven't delivered the ashes of my father to the bay he so dearly loved.

Friendship Sealed

M Y SUMMER TRAVELS take me to the island of Catalina off the California coast. Generally I'll spend several months anchored in various coves on the lee side of the island taking pictures, spearfishing, and living off the sea as best I can. This summer after anchoring my sloop in a new cove, I discovered several harbor seals occupying a section of protruding boulders a hundred yards west of my anchorage.

In the early mornings and evenings they hunted along the extended points of the cove, working the kelp beds for fish. Several times I tried to join them, but when I neared, they bolted off in a rush and disappeared into the thick mesh of the kelp forest. Not wishing to press, and figuring I had plenty of time to ease my way into their uncomplicated life, I let it be. It was early summer and I had other fish to fry; the yellowtail were starting to show and the white sea bass were running strong.

The spearfishing was good up near the west end of the island, and enroute to that far point, I came upon a large colony of harbor seals a mile east of a white sea bass bed. The harbor seal colonies around the island are quite small, rarely more than a half dozen to an area. Here there were eleven seals dozing on separate boulders close to the shoreline.

A mature harbor seal comes in various shades of brown, though their coats appear charcoal when wet. The adolescents are of this charcoal color as are most of the newborns, save for the prematures which are often white with black spots. Marked as they are, the adults, while resting on boulders, are difficult to see from a distance. Usually they can be spotted in the water, their slick, black heads contrasting the silver surface and looking for all the world like a pack of labrador retrievers looking for a lost stick.

Intrigued by the large colony, I decided to try and make contact, reasoning that their numbers would favor a better opportunity. It was midday and I approached after having speared two bonito, a three pounder and an eight pounder, so that I might bribe my way into their good graces. Anchoring my skiff fifty yards away, I entered the water and swam slowly toward the sleeping seals. One by one they rose from their sleeping positions and intently followed my movements. When I was within thirty feet of the nearest seal, it slipped off its rock. This was followed by an avalanche of seals as the remainder of the colony hit the water.

Holding a fish in each hand I expected the seals to come in and inspect as sea lions often do. But they only gave quick peeks, half-hidden behind kelp stalks. Hanging in an open space surrounded by kelp, I waited. Every so often I dropped down to the bottom offering the bonito to any takers. Another five minutes passed before an adult slipped up from behind and began sniffing my fins. When I turned to it, the seal darted away glancing suspiciously over its shoulder before disappearing into the haze. Shortly, a round butterball of a seal, the largest of the colony and probably the alpha male, came boldly forward and extended its clawed flippers. Ever so gently it took the large bonito from my hand and swam away. Encouraged by the gesture, I hung around another twenty minutes. But no other seal come forward, so I deposited the bonito on one of the rocks and left.

Twice during the following week I returned to the colony and the pattern was the same. When I neared the seals, they dashed off in the same fashion, leaving me waving a fish in empty water. The alpha male, though it made passes, did not take the fish. Not a seal thereafter accepted my offerings. Perhaps a seal etiquette, of which I was ignorant, had been broken. Bribery was no way to begin a relationship. I desired to make legitimate contact with a wild creature on its terms. Instead I had insulted it with an easy meal that smacked of Sea World.

Having lost face with this colony, I elected to concentrate on the smaller colony near my anchorage. The first two visits turned up empty; nobody home. The third visit found the seals back on their boulders and I approached empty handed.

Treading water twenty feet from the nearest adult, I watched it watch me from its dry perch. Oddly, it didn't leap from its rock into the protective custody of the water. Instead, a small seal closer to shore slipped off its rock and, as seals were in the habit of doing, took a circular route and came up behind me to sniff my fins. Hanging unmoving in the water, I allowed the seal to thoroughly inspect me. Satisfied, it swam around for a clear view of my face. Slowly I made a dive to the shallow bottom. The seal followed, then rocketed by me and turned to wait on the bottom, turning onto its back and spreading its flippers as if to say, "Why do you move so slowly?"

Returning to the surface for a breath, the seal was at my side; it wanted to play. I was at once befuddled and ecstatic with the actions of my friend.

Down again, the seal swam parallel with me along the sandy bottom. Face to face we looked into the other's eyes. When I tried to get closer it moved away, maintaining a distance of four feet.

The freedom of diving without scuba allowed me to sustain contact when the seal made its dashes of abandoned play. But it would always have to turn and wait for me to catch up, encouraging me to hurry with impatient gestures of head turning and barrel rolls, as if there was only so much time in a day to play, and I was pitifully wasting it away.

I also had the sensation of being tested so that the seal might understand better how much play I was capable of enduring. I'm sure I was a disappointment. For I was woefully bereft in swimming skills, and hopelessly short of a breath-hold that my friend would consider to be marginal at best.

The seal was becoming bored with me, and to make matters worse, we had drifted into deeper water where the vigorous action shortened my bottom time still further. I tried to entice it back to the shallows, but it was reluctant to follow. After forty minutes of play, it wandered off leaving me gasping on the surface.

Three times in the next week I made contact with the same gray seal. We played as before, one on one, with the seal maintaining an arm's length distance between us. Never could I get closer than that invisible barrier. Whenever I extended my arm to sneak a touch, it moved. It moved when its back was turned, it moved in blind spots from below and on top. It knew something I didn't know, and would never know. Or maybe I did know it, but didn't know that I knew it.

On one occasion I brought a female diver to the colony for a photo session. The additional diver changed the mix, and though the seal did not bolt off, it kept a distance of twelve feet. Why twelve and not ten or eight or sixteen? I have no way of knowing. But it was always twelve. In an attempt to get shots that included both the diver and the seal, the continual maneuvering made the seal leery, and on two occasions I penetrated its "safe zone," and it bared its teeth and made a lunge at me clearly communicating my violation. It was the first aggressive gesture a harbor seal had shown and it was absolutely correct. The action was not enough to discourage play, but it clearly established the twelve-foot boundaries. When we moved into shallow water and I inadvertently pushed the seal close to shore, giving it no route of escape, it lunged again. And again it was perfectly correct in its communication. I thought that I might have pushed our relationship too far, but when I ran out of film and was returning to the boat, it followed us most of the way back before returning to the warmth of its dry rock.

Over the course of the summer I visited my friend a couple of times every week and played, as always, but could get no nearer than four feet. One afternoon into the third month, two new seals were swimming in the area, a white yearling with black spots and its full-grown mother. I did my usual routine of hanging and waiting for them to come in and sniff my fins. The white seal came up immediately, sniffed, then swung around and faced me, making direct eye contact. The mother kept her distance and seemed unconcerned with my presence. There have been times in the past when aggressive lunges have been made by protective sea lions towards divers who have swum too close to their pups, but this mother harbor seal had apparently given permission to play.

The white seal showed no evidence of fear or caution. When I dove, it dove, and when I came up for air, it came up for air. Soon we were swimming upside down, doing hangs, spins and whatever else I could think up. Then, while on the surface recapturing my breath, the seal came up to me face to face, and without much thought, more as a reflex act, I reached out to touch it. It didn't move away as I brushed its chest. It moved closer. The brush turned into stroking. The impenetrable barrier had suddenly, inexplicably been crossed as naturally as could be imagined. I removed my glove so I could feel the luxuriant coat. The fur was slick and soft at the same time. The white seal draped one of its clawed flippers over my extended arm and we floated there in the water like formal dancers pirouetting to music only we could hear.

It didn't last very long; the young seal was anxious to get on with the fun of being a seal and broke away to continue the ballet under the water. Though the moment was brief, it crystallized inside of me. The experience was unlike anything that could be found in our civilized world, and its effect was powerful. The distance between me and the natural world closed a bit more tightly; in those moments in fact, it embraced me. I cannot name the thing that happens to a human when he or she is touched by a wild animal. It is a powerful connection, and forever changes a person. Somehow all the world becomes momentarily perfect, as if it was always so.

c. e.
Summer of '84

Lobster Museum

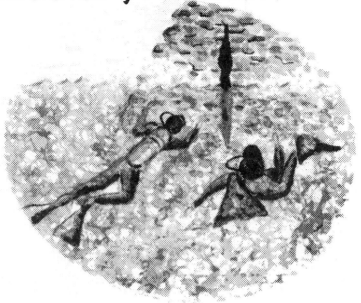

AN AFTERNOON WESTERLY kicked white caps off the sun dappled Catalina channel. Allen McGee, in his wetsuit, leaned over the railing of the green-trimmed Avalon public pier on Catalina Island. Stocky and broad shouldered, his dark hair lay wet and matted, framing his youthful face. Without looking at the Dive Shack to his left where both his and Wayne Stewart's tanks were being filled, he said, "It's getting pretty rough out there. No sense in pounding our guts out going against it. We'll have to stay inside and dive Frog Rock, or someplace close."

"It doesn't make any difference to me," replied Stewart who was in the Dive Shack. Stewart was a head taller than McGee and expressed a perpetual child-like wonder from wide-set blue eyes. "We aren't going to find lobster anyway."

McGee leaned into the Dive Shack and tapped the shoulder of a local teenager who was filling the tanks. "We've come up empty this whole week. You know any good lobster spots on this side of the island? We only got four days left."

The teenager, bored to dullness from his task replied, "You know how many times I get asked that question? All I do is fill up tanks, Bud, I don't have time to..." He paused for a moment and gazed down the pier towards the hamburger stand. "Hey, listen, if you want to find the really good spots, go ask that old guy walking by the hamburger stand. He knows every lobster hole on the island. He's been diving here for about fifty years."

"That white-haired guy?" asked McGee.

"Yeah, that's him, Frank Baumgartner. But don't say I put you on to him. He's a crusty old fart, can't stand tourists."

McGee stared for a moment at the stocky, bowlegged man shuffling down the pier. "We got nothing to lose," he said beginning to walk towards the old man.

Behind him the teenager from the Dive Shack called, "Don't tell him I sent you."

Stewart was a step behind when McGee gained the old man's side. McGee cleared his throat and Baumgartner made a half turn, his gray, muttonchop beard further accentuating his round, deeply lined, face. Intense, silverblue eyes housed in pockets of flesh sharply scrutinized the young men before him.

"Mr. Baumgartner," said McGee, "we heard you really know the good dive spots around the island. We were wondering if you could give us an idea where we could pick up a couple of lobsters?"

Baumgartner shot a glance at the Dive Shack then back to McGee. "I can't help you," he said, then turned to continue his way down the pier towards the street.

McGee and Stewart trotted up beside him.

"Listen, Mr. Baumgartner, we'll pay you," said Stewart.

Baumgartner's pace did not slacken. "You don't have enough money, boys."

"Then we'll work. You got anything that needs fixing, or moved or something. You need a hand with some heavy work. We'll do anything," pleaded McGee.

Baumgartner stopped. "Listen boys, you don't get it. It's not the money. It's not the work. Right now I could use some help hauling my skiff out of the water. I've got to clean and paint the bottom. But I wouldn't trade you what I know for any amount of money or work. There ain't that many lobsters or abalone left. If I put you onto the spot, you'd take all you could get your hands on. If anything was left you'd go home and brag about it to your friends and show them pictures. Then you'd swear your best dive buddy to secrecy and tell him where to find the spot. He'd tell somebody else, and come next fall there wouldn't be a lobster left. That's the way it works."

Baumgartner started for the street again.

"We wouldn't tell anyone," said Stewart. "We'd take only the legal limit. We're here from Oregon. Anyone we'd tell would never get down here to dive these spots. We'll probably never get down here again ourselves. This is our last year of college, our last shot at some freedom before we..."

"Sorry boys," interrupted Baumgartner. "I've heard all them reasons before. Better ones than yours, and it always ends up the same; everything winds up gettin' cleaned out. You boys are wasting your time."

Baumgartner hit the street and left McGee and Stewart standing in small puddles that dripped from their wet suits.

"So now what?" asked Stewart.

"So now we decide if we want lobsters fresh out of the ocean or served up to us in a restaurant," replied McGee.

"You got something in mind?"

"Let's go back to the Dive Shack and see if that guy knows which skiff belongs to Baumgartner."

In the late afternoon of the following day McGee and Stewart were sitting atop the railing of the pier next to the hamburger stand when Baumgartner strode by. He spotted them and smiled a thin smile.

"You two must want to eat lobster mighty bad to pull a man's skiff out of the water without his permission, then clean and paint the bottom. I'm much obliged, that's a full day's job for one man."

"We give our word," said McGee, "we won't take more than our limit. And we won't say where we got them."

Baumgartner nodded his head in mild acquiescence. "Well, you were willing to take a chance on me, I guess I can take one with you. You got a boat?"

"We got a Whaler for the rest of the week."

"All right. You know most folks don't realize that the only good lobster holes left are in shallow water. Illegal traps and scuba divers took all there was in deep water."

McGee looked at Stewart then at Baumgartner. "We been using scuba gear."

"And that's why you haven't got any lobster. None of that gear is going to do you any good where I'm going to send you," said Baumgartner. "You're going to have to free dive for 'em."

"If it's in shallow water, we can handle it," said McGee with Stewart nodding in agreement.

Baumgartner grinned and nodded back. "Maybe. You know where to find the cove called Italian Gardens?"

"Sure," said Stewart, "we've been there."

"Well you go about a mile past there, to that small cove just before Twin Rocks. You know where I'm talking about?"

"I think so," said McGee.

"At the east side of the cove the island drops straight down into the water, sheer cliff. There's a couple of little jags of rock in there, and one cave that rises out of the water thirty feet at high tide. Right next to it are two smaller caves that barely break water at low tide. They're completely submerged at high tide. The far cave, the one furthest west, is full of lobsters, big ones. It's only ten feet deep, but the cave's black as coal dust. Take a light with you, and don't go in if there's a west swell running. You could get jammed up in there."

Stewart and McGee were all smiles. "Thanks Mr. Baumgartner. We'll hit it tomorrow morning bright and early. We'll let you know how we do."

"Yeah boys, you do that," said Baumgartner, smiling.

The morning was windless and the sea was flat and smooth as a billiard table. McGee and Stewart rode west up the island taking their bearings off Twin Rocks and reached the cove in forty minutes. Drifting along the east end they easily spotted the high cave in the cliff and dropped anchor.

McGee led the way to the far cave that, with each gentle surge, forced air out its creviced roof like a congested exhale from the island itself. The cave was in ten feet of water and the entrance was but a thin slit that would scarcely accommodate a single diver. McGee switched on his light and leaned into the entrance, squeezing in up to his waist. He ran the beam around the walls of what was more a tunnel than a cave, then dropped it down to the pit where scrambled more lobsters than he had ever seen in one place. The lobsters were all enormous, ranging between seven and twelve pounds. It was as if he had stumbled into a cave that had miraculously been overlooked by the twentieth century. It was as though he were peering back into a time when the ocean floor around the island must have been littered with lobsters. The sighting pulled the breath from his lungs, and he pushed his shoulders back through the narrow opening and floated to the surface. "They're in here! Take a look!" He handed the light to Stewart who lowered himself into the opening and pushed halfway through.

In twenty seconds he popped back up to the surface.

"Man, what a sight. Did you ever think you'd see something like that! There must have been thirty or forty bugs in there! They were huge!"

Stewart paused as if to fully comprehend the spectacle he had just witnessed. Then he said, "Well you got us here, you should take the first bug."

"Okay," said McGee. "The cave's a tight fit and narrows down toward the back. Keep an eye on me. If I get stuck be ready to pull me out."

Stewart nodded as McGee began to hyperventilate. After taking several deep breaths he lowered himself to the entrance and squeezed through the slit, his weight belt catching on the side and momentarily halting him halfway through. He pushed his way clear, and hooked one of his fins to the outside edge of the entrance so he wouldn't drift untethered deeper inside. The cave was tight and angled sharply off to the left, tapering severely to a dead-end wedge fifteen feet away. McGee swept the light down the tunnel's length, spooking the lobsters into full retreat, then brought the beam back to a single lobster that was still frozen to the wall and was within reaching distance. Lunging for it, he gripped the lobster atop its carapace and drew it to his chest. Immediately the lobster's tail began to flail wildly and McGee's single hand-hold was not enough to contain it. The lobster sprung from his grasp, and bounced into other lobsters, stampeding them deeper into the cave. The sudden action stole the last of McGee's breath and he anxiously made his way out and wiggled through the opening. Exploding to the surface, and between gasps of breath, he told Stewart what had happened.

Stewart took the light, and after several deep inhales slipped between the edges of the opening, pushing his way down the tunnel a full body-length until his fins hooked to the entrance of the cave. The lobsters had crowded down into the dead end of the tunnel and were hanging on the walls and ceiling, and crawling over one another on the floor. He could reach the nearest lobster if he unhooked his fins from the cave opening and moved forward another three feet. But in the narrow tunnel he would be unable to turn around, and would have to back out blindly at the end of his breath-hold. It was a risk he was unwilling to take, even for a ten-pound lobster, and so wormed his way back out the entrance.

Reaching the surface he treaded water with McGee. "They've all gone down to the end of the passageway. This isn't going to be as easy as Baumgartner made it out to be."

"Yeah," replied McGee. "I think he knew what he was doing. It's too tight for a scuba rig, so it has to be free dived. It's not so deep that we can't hold our breaths. He knew it'd come down to balls."

"Maybe one of us should go in first, and the other follow as far as he can, keeping contact with the opening, and be ready to pull the lead guy out if he gets in trouble."

"So who's going to be the lead guy?" asked McGee full well knowing the answer.

"You've got a better breath-hold than me. You've done more free diving."

"Stay close behind."

Both McGee and Stewart hyperventilated, and when they inhaled their last breath, submerged in sync. McGee entered the cave, pulled himself through, released his fins from the opening, and turned down the tunnel. Stewart followed, keeping a hand-hold on the tip of McGee's fins. Once into the passageway McGee had to fight to control the claustrophobia that was rising in his chest. The lobsters had moved down to the end of the tunnel, and were further away than before. Inching his way down the narrowing tunnel, he reached the nearest lobster and threw the beam of light into its eyes and snatched it from the wall. He tried to swing it into his body, but the motion rolled him into a half turn that had him facing the rock wall an inch from his mask. It was enough to unleash the panic that had fluttered under his throat, and he dropped the lobster and frantically began pushing his way backward towards the entrance. Stewart knew something had gone wrong and tried to pull on McGee's fins, but couldn't without first easing back out the opening and getting a good hand-hold at the entrance. When finally he found leverage, he was able to back out and pull McGee with him.

In the open air they both lifted their masks from their faces and gulped in breaths; then without a word, turned and swam for the anchored boat.

The boys hung around the hamburger stand all afternoon waiting for Baumgartner to show up. In the late afternoon he came shuffling up, all smiles. "How'd you boys make out?"

"We found the cave Mr. Baumgartner," said McGee, "and saw a bunch of lobsters, but they hauled ass back in that tunnel and we couldn't get them." McGee paused. "You figured that's what would happen. It wasn't very fair Mr. Baumgartner."

"Now hold on boys. You wanted lobsters, and I put you on to a spot. A good diver could have taken all he wanted. Fair's got nothing to do with it."

"I don't think any diver could have gotten those lobsters. Not one," said Stewart angrily. "You'd have to be King Neptune to get those lobsters."

Baumgartner saw betrayal in the boys faces. He had set them up for failure, and they willingly obliged. He sighed a breath and nodded his head.

"All right boys, tell you what. We'll all go back tomorrow morning and see what we can do. I'll meet you here on the pier at eight o'clock."

Baumgartner had little to say during the forty minute boat ride, and the boys, taking their cue, held their tongues despite a welling of anticipation. After anchoring in the same spot they pulled out their gear and suited up. Baumgartner's wet suit was a sight to behold. There were chunks of neoprene missing or flapping loose, bare spaces showed skin at the knees and elbows. He used old style UDT swim fins that looked like they'd been issued during World War II. His face mask was old and the back strap was so rotten, it looked like a spider web when he stretched it over his head. His snorkel was of a recent model, but his weight belt was one that must have been found on the bottom of the sea because barnacles and old sea growth were encrusted everywhere. He wore leather gloves and carried no knife. The boys were witnessing a breed that had all but vanished from the sea and they simultaneously sensed history and loss. In Baumgartner's sure movements they also realized something special was about to occur.

"One of you boys carry that old bag of mine, and I'll take your light."

He slipped over the side of the boat with scarcely a ripple.

McGee and Stewart were taken by surprise at the suddenness of his move, and had to rush to catch up. By the time they reached the entrance to the cave, Baumgartner was backing out with a ten pound lobster pressed to his chest. Stewart, who had the bag, stared in open awe as Baumgartner waited for him to regain his senses and open the bag to deposit the lobster. He went back into the cave, and in twenty seconds reappeared with another, equally as big as the first. On his third dive McGee followed him into the cave and watched him turn the corner into the tunnel, his light beam moving half way down before stopping at a lobster that the light beam had mesmerized to the wall. He grabbed it and with the tail flailing away, backed out of the tunnel. McGee, who was leaning through the opening, had to scramble to get out of Baumgartner's way. Outside the entrance of the tunnel, Baumgartner reappeared and dropped the third lobster into the bag. In five minutes time the bag held thirty pounds of lobster. Barely taking time to catch a breath, Baumgartner dove back into the cave. McGee trailed and watched him pull his way down the tunnel that was now nearly empty of lobsters. At the tunnel's very end, Baumgartner made a turn, and save for the reflection of his light, disappeared from sight. Apparently at the end of the tunnel there was another room that was large enough to make a turn. For after a long moment, Baumgartner came head first through the passageway carrying a lobsters under one arm and had a second pinned to his chest. Giving way, McGee backed out and resurfaced. Seconds later Baumgartner emerged and released the two lobsters into the waiting bag. Treading water, he took his snorkel from his mouth. "That ought to do us, boys. One for me, two for each of you. Unless of course you boys can eat more than twenty pounds of lobster at one sitting. Both McGee and Stewart smiled at his little joke, and then looked into the bag; yet unable to fully comprehend the feat that had just been displayed. So sure and fearlessly did Baumgartner operate in the ocean, so effortlessly did he capture the lobsters, that the entire event hardly seemed real: A quick dream where one awakes to a bag full of the biggest lobsters one has ever seen, or would ever hope to see.

On their return to the green pier at Avalon, Baumgartner reminded them of their agreement. "I trust you boy's will keep this place to yourselves." Then he paused and looked back at the cove that was fading into the configurations of the island. Almost to himself he said, "Look at this as a visit to an ocean museum where they keep a few things that don't exist anymore. A place to remind us how things were, just a few years back."

Spooked

To allay their fears of the awesome powers of the natural world, primitive peoples sanctified these powers through the creation and worship of totems with the idea that the powers would become benevolent, if they were accorded the proper respect. Thus the sun god and rain god were born, as were significant animal deities; among them the bear and buffalo, serpent and shark. Here in the late twentieth century, those gods have been long abandoned, or at the very least, buried deep in our subconscious; all but one "the shark" the sea god. The sea god lives in modern man, as the most fearsome gods once lived in primitive peoples. Its face is not carved on totems or etched in rock, but it resides in the caves of big-screen movie theaters and in the household totems we call television. We flock in worship to the larger-than-life faces on the big screen. It is where we go to probe the unknown and sometimes dangerous world that lurks in the hidden recesses of our ancient minds. That same dark country also resides beneath the surfaces of our oceans and seas. The metaphor is inescapable.

We fear the shark with the same loathing that we fear death and all the unknowns it holds for us. When measured against the dangers of our times, the fear of sharks appears as irrational as a preoccupation with lightening bolts. To know that the automobile has killed more in a single day than the combined shark attacks on divers for the past fifty years, puts this ill-founded fear in perspective. So while there is no real logic to our fears when held up against the realities of day to day living, we must conclude that the fear exists largely because it is sustained on the silver-screened walls of our modern day caves and in the totems of books and television. For as advanced as we may think we are, when it comes to the shark there is little distance between us and our primitive brothers and sisters.

Despite our culture's persuasive shark mythology, not all have succumbed to the images that flicker out across the darkened movie houses. There are those among us who have transcended the shark myths, and indeed, have, after a fashion, done battle with the shark. They are the dragon slayers of our time who defy the myths of the deep unknown and plunge headlong into its belly. These men are not fools. They go with no illusions; they know the shark is real, and exists beyond the movie theaters, and can suddenly appear out of the blue haze more awesome than was ever captured on the silver screen.

Take the case of Harry Ingram, a modern day dragon slayer. (The following is excerpted from the book, *The Last of the Blue Water Hunters.*) It was late afternoon, and the water was dirty, thirty to forty feet of visibility, which by any other standard is decent water, but here in these normally crystal clear waters where the visibility exceeds a hundred feet, it was considered poor. Tom Blanford took his short gun into the water in search of yellowtail for dinner. In almost no time he strung a large blue fin tuna, close to a hundred pounds. Without the flotation that a tuna rig provides, he had no chance at the fish, and those in the boat saw him plowing across the water for some seventy feet before the five hundred pound test line broke or was severed.

"Tuna", he yelled. And Harry Ingram and two other divers suited up while Tom returned to get his tuna rig. Within twenty minutes Tom had speared another tuna, this one smaller, maybe sixty pounds. The blue fin tore off like a runaway freight train when struck by the spear. Tom returned to the surface and watched the line zip out from his double floated rig. Suddenly the tension relaxed and the line slacked. He gave it a pull to test the fish, but there was nothing on the other end. Apparently the tuna had pulled out. Not unusual. The soft flesh of the fish combined with its tremendous power make it the most difficult of all fish in the ocean to land. Reluctantly, Tom drew in his line while swimming in the direction the tuna had been heading. Sixty feet from the point of his initial contact with the fish, a ball of blood six feet in diameter hung in the water, far too much blood for the wound of a spear to produce. Odd, thought Tom, I wonder what happened?

He continued to pull in his shooting line and restring his speargun. Harry, meanwhile, had drifted away and was fifty feet or so outside of Tom. Knowing that tuna had moved into the area lifted Harry to that level of ultra-alertness that is generated when a hunter is aware that big game is on the move. He was looking intently in all directions when beneath him swam the shark.

"It came from behind me and on the right. It was turned slightly on its right side and from twenty feet down looked straight up at me with its left eye. My first thought when I saw its massive girth was, 'I'm a dead man'. There was no doubt that it was a great white shark. Later we figured that by its length, somewhere between fifteen and twenty feet, it must have weighed well over three thousand pounds. But at the time, none of that registered in me. I lifted my head out of the water and yelled 'shark', because I wanted the others to know what had killed me. I'd been diving blue water for eight years and I'd seen sharks, but the sight of this enormous creature completely unnerved me. Then it swam about fifty feet away and I thought, maybe I have a chance, maybe it will circle. As the thought cleared my head the shark turned and headed right for me. It covered the fifty feet and was on top of me with its mouth open in half a second."

Several divers on the boat had heard Harry's shark cry and could see him floating on the surface. Then they saw Harry suddenly thrust backward, lifted waist high and spun out of the water. Ten feet of the expansive back of the shark erupted out of the water (they never saw the head or tail) just in front of him, and they saw Harry fall across it in a cascade of thrashing white water. It was as shocking a sight as a blue water hunter could see; but for circumstance, it could have been anyone in the boat. To all who witnessed the assault, it was assumed that Harry had been bitten in half. There was no way he could have survived the attack.

In a last act of desperation Harry pulled the trigger on his speargun and then the shark hit him. He doesn't remember the next few moments. Apparently the shark took the fired arrow plus four feet of spear stock, with the last foot of spear stock perhaps being all that stood between Harry and the mouth of the great white. Miraculously, he was not bitten. The force of the shark's momentum drove the butt of the speargun into his left shoulder, spun and lifted him just out of reach of the jaws. As the shark broke water, he fell across the great white's head and rolled over its left eye. Then they both slipped back into the water. The shark turned and struck for the open ocean, dragging the tuna rig and leaving Harry unscathed save for a deep bruise on his left shoulder.

The extraordinary thing about that story, aside from the fact that Harry lived, is that he is still diving the blue water - I suspect though that he may not be the same diver he once was. "Often," he says, "when I am out there working the drop offs, dangling as vulnerable as a puppet, I see that shark swimming out of the haze."

Despite the playback, Harry hangs tough and goes about his underwater business; though sometimes he gets angry that the great white hit him, because it now swims in his mind. And when that happens you cannot be totally free in the water. The great white stole his ocean freedom. That is what the shark myth does to the divers who play that shark-filled mind tape while in the water; it steals their ability to operate freely in the ocean.

The diver that has always had that shark tape running doesn't really understand what has been taken. He doesn't know what it's like to move about the underwater environment unencumbered by the weight of his shark anxiety. His attention is divided between the ocean and the sea god of the silver screen, and he misses the beauty that is before his eyes. The sharks that swim in the mind hold far more terror and are infinitely more restrictive to the diver than the sharks which swim in the seas.

There is sometimes a fine line between the sharks of the seas and the sharks of one's mind. Omar Wood, a fearless hunter of his day once told me that his most terrifying moment came after he had speared a large rooster fish down in the Sea of Cortez, many years ago when there was still an abundance of sharks cruising those waters. He had gut shot the fish, and by the time he had a hand on it, the thing was thrashing and whipping its guts and blood everywhere. Omar couldn't see a thing for the turbulence, and it freaked him out because he could feel something with razor sharp teeth torpedoing into him, biting anything that moved. Long moments brought him alongside the boat and eventual clear water. There was no sign of shark anywhere; all was quiet. All his terror was a creation of the mind, born out of real events. It has happened to us all. Even the dragon slayers are not immune. On the other hand, they do see more sharks and are more alert to the possibilities of an encounter when a wounded fish is thrashing about.

Which brings me to another shark story of my own. While spending time on a remote island in the Fijian archipelago, I had fallen into the habit of casually pulling up wounded fish while the gathering white tip reef sharks circled in quick darting movements around it. Always when the fish was within ten feet of me the sharks would break off and disappear back into the depths, leaving me with the over-confident belief that their behavior was predictable.

Then came the day when I speared a large coral trout that had holed up in seventy feet of water. While making repeated dives to extract it, a half dozen white tips began to circle the area. When I finally freed up the fish and began my swim for the surface the shark numbers had doubled. They twitched and turned, and one got so bold as to brush my leg in its attempt to get to the fish. All confidence drained, I unhesitatingly let go of the fish, but the spearfisherman in me still held on to the line to which it was attached.

On the surface, and twenty feet above the frenzy, I swam to the nearest reef and climbed clear out of the water, standing fearlessly ankle deep several yards from the drop off. I then pulled the line with the attached fish up to the reef thinking that the sharks would turn away once they were in shallow water. Wrong. They came right up and on to the reef, biting air and reef in an attempt to get to the fish. What bravado was left vanished as I desperately tried to poke and kick the fish back over the drop off. Some blue water hunter, some dragon slayer. I waited there on my perch until the line went slack, then cautiously reentered the water. All was calm, no sign of sharks, no sign of the coral trout, just the naked spearshaft twisting in the light current. Suffice it to say, my cavalier approach to reef sharks changed considerably. They were given their proper respect, and never again will I allow a fish to hole up on me.

Attacks by reef sharks are rare. The few divers that are bitten are, for the most part, spearfishermen who are bitten by accident. Art Pinder in Florida, considered by many to be the best who ever lived, has been bitten five times; by reef sharks attempting to get to the fish he had either strung to him or was bringing up just after spearing it.

There are basically two kinds of sharks that swim in the oceans and seas: 1) prehistoric beasts, and 2) all others, including reef sharks, blues, makos, hammerheads and any shark under ten feet long. How can you tell the difference? I guess it depends to a degree on your time and experience in the water. To some, a harmless leopard shark could appear prehistoric. I suppose the rule is: If you gotta ask if it was prehistoric, then it wasn't. A great white is a prehistoric beast. To my knowledge, the only deadly encounters with sharks have been with great whites. In those cases it was simply the spearfisherman's misfortune to be in the same water at the time a great white passed through. Some have escaped the jaws of a great white, as Harry did, others have not.

I have never seen a great white in the water, but I have seen a prehistoric beast in the water. I was laying on the surface off a deep water reef in the South Pacific waiting for tuna. In the two hundred foot visibility there appeared a whale swimming along the outside edge of the reef. It was coming at a high rate of speed, directly towards me. Within moments I recognized the whale to be a shark. A very, very big shark. It must have been at least twenty five feet long. It was kind of a dark mustardbrown, and had a black strip near its tail. Its arching pectoral fins were four feet long and it had a body that looked five feet across. In its entirety – twelve to thirteen feet wide. There was no guessing the weight of such a creature; it was beyond my scope. It had a remora clamped just in front of its massive dorsal fin, and the remora looked five feet long. I am not sure to this day whether it was the size of the shark or the speed with which it moved, or both, but the sighting of it literally paralyzed me in the water.

Frozen on the surface, it moved beneath me at a depth of forty feet, turned to its side and eyed me once then banked off in one fluid motion to deep water, without ever a movement of tail or fin. In that moment I was reduced to one of those minute water skimmers that you see on the surface of lakes and streams in the early spring before the trout eat them. My speargun felt puny and worthless. The spearshaft wouldn't have made that shark blink. I was on ice. A moment in the water with such a beast captures more of its reality than any movie could ever hope to convey. The sea god had come to pay me a visit and I was appropriately humbled.

In the days that followed I played it very cautious on the deep outside. I twisted and turned looking for the shark, waiting for it to reappear. After a while I realized that I had been running a very old tape with a new picture in my head. The shark-myth tape that every diver runs whenever they get the "spooked" feeling in unfamiliar water, or deep water that's hazy, or "shark-infested waters" or any water, for that matter that becomes uncomfortable.

In truth, everyone is susceptible to that "spooked" feeling from time to time. Even the blue water hunters, who must live by their ocean instincts, will slide into the water and declare to themselves that "it just doesn't feel right." Often there is no accounting for the feeling; it hits you that something is wrong. And so following his gut, as every good hunter must, he gets out of the water and moves to another spot. He does this because he knows that one cannot operate effectively in the ocean with a shark tape running amok in ones head.

There are many for whom the shark-myth tape never stops playing. And, regrettably, those divers will eventually be driven from the water, never to dive again. More is the shame because overcoming this self-created anxiety is not as difficult as it might seem.

There are basically two methods that I have found useful in eliminating the shark tape from my mind. One is obvious: Simply move into water where you are feeling comfortable. If that is in ten feet, fine. There, at least, one can operate with faculties intact and enjoy the ocean in all its splendor. The second method calls for a bit of de-programming. If you must dive in unfamiliar water and cannot move to a more comfortable environment, and the shark tape begins its tune, become aware of its source. Tell yourself that it is a creation of the mind and nothing more, then force it from your thoughts with a tad bit of anger. Each time the shark surfaces assure yourself that you are being manipulated by a modern day mythology, and then let it go. If the feeling persists, get out of the water, but do not bend to the mythology. If you de-program every time that shark swims into your head you'll eventually free yourself from that anxiety-inducing tape. As you do, your diving experience will change from a closed-off internal ordeal to a joyful adventure of new discovery.

There is a third method, the way of the Masai warrior of the East African plain. Before the twentieth century turned the Masai into a herdsman, he passed into manhood by overcoming his deepest fears of the wild, by trekking out into the field with only spear and shield to single-handedly kill a fully grown lion. So, if you must, select a proper speargun, and travel to those deep, tuna-filled waters off Guadalupe Island in the Pacific, Harry Ingram can show you the spot; slide into the water and just hang out there for a while and wait.

c.e.
fall '91

Techniques of Snorkeling

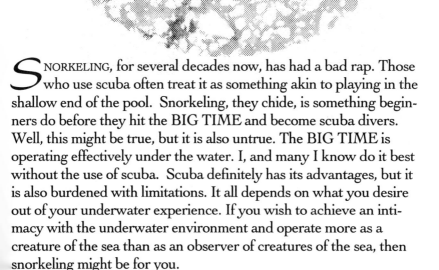

SNORKELING, for several decades now, has had a bad rap. Those who use scuba often treat it as something akin to playing in the shallow end of the pool. Snorkeling, they chide, is something beginners do before they hit the BIG TIME and become scuba divers. Well, this might be true, but it is also untrue. The BIG TIME is operating effectively under the water. I, and many I know do it best without the use of scuba. Scuba definitely has its advantages, but it is also burdened with limitations. It all depends on what you desire out of your underwater experience. If you wish to achieve an intimacy with the underwater environment and operate more as a creature of the sea than as an observer of creatures of the sea, then snorkeling might be for you.

Snorkeling can be as easy as it can be demanding. There are surprisingly few limitations in terms of what can be accomplished on a breath-hold dive. Only the bottom is the limit.

The ocean world is sensitive to sound and movement. Thus it becomes the snorkelers's purpose to move without appearing to move and to do it soundlessly. The first rule of snorkeling in the ocean is to become conscious of every sound and movement you make, however slight they might be.

Listen to yourself; the splash of the fins, the sound of your breath through the snorkel tube, the contact of any hard objects, (a knife against a weight, a weight against a rock.) Breathe easy through a large diameter snorkel. Does your breath whistle? Does it chug, or wheeze? The more open the mouth and throat, the quieter the breaths. Listen carefully, remembering that sound is carried five times farther under the water than in the air.

For the beginning snorkeler controlling movement is difficult. The ocean seems to be pushing us all over the place and there is a tendency to over-use arms and legs to maintain equilibrium. But once you get a feel for the ocean and begin to relax, then greater awareness of body movement becomes possible. Avoid thrashing around on the surface, and maintain an even flutter kick that is below the surface. Keep your arms to your side and glide whenever possible. The best advice I ever received when it came to breath-hold diving was not to force anything. Move where it is easy to move. Dive to depths that are comfortable. Stay comfortable and relaxed at all times and let the ocean come to you.

The breath-hold underwater is overrated. It's not how long you can hold your breath, but how smooth you're able to operate when you're down. There is a lot of talk, both negative and positive regarding hyperventilation; the flushing of stale air out of the lungs and gorging the blood with oxygen before taking a final breath. Really all you need is a few deep breaths, no more than three. If you begin to feel at all dizzy then cut it back to two or even one. Practice in shallow water and get a feel for your own capacity. Find your limits and stay within them. Efficient use of energy is the most effective way to sustain bottom time. Relaxation, above all else, determines bottom time. So dive within the boundaries of your own personal "comfort zone". If you are not enjoying the dive, you're probably out of your comfort zone. If you are enjoying your dive, then you can be reasonably assured that you are being economical with the fixed amount of oxygen you're holding in your lungs. When you come up from a dive, give yourself time to recapture your breath, and relax until your breaths are even and controlled. This period may be just a few minutes or as much as five minutes. Test it out and discover where it suits you. Remember that your bottom time is more a product of relaxations than of lung capacity.

Think of snorkeling as a sort of horizontal martial art. Every movement has a purpose and all action is coordinated into flowing clean movements. Keeping this martial art in mind there are basically two methods for quietly submerging your body under the water; the jackknife dive and the feet-first drop.

While floating on the surface the jackknife dive is made by bending at the waist 90 degrees and then dropping down. As your upper body goes under, pull your legs up as though you were about to go into a hand-stand, then allow the lower portion of the body to follow the torso straight down into the water. No need to kick your feet until your fins are completely submerged. Then use only enough kicks to initiate a glide.

The feet first dive is used primarily in thick kelp, where only the more experienced diver should find himself. Use the weight of your upper body instead of your legs to begin the dive. Pushing with your hands and kicking with your fins, raise yourself high out of the water, then stop kicking and allow the weight of your raised body to send you down feet first. Once under the water bend at the waist, turn and kick yourself down.

The surface dive is perhaps the most critical because it sets up the rest of the dive. If it is quiet and smooth in all likelihood so will be the dive. Just before a dive I'll pull the snorkel from my mouth to prevent noisy bubbles from exiting on descent. Then, upon ascent I replace the snorkel in my mouth, round off the ascent, blowing as the top of my head is parallel with the surface for an easy exhale. Develop the techniques for both the descent and ascent until they become a smooth, and noiseless art that has rhythm and feels absolutely natural.

Breath-hold diving creates the necessity for a great many more pressure equalizations in your ears and sinuses than does scuba diving. For those unfamiliar with this procedure, equalizing your middle ear and sinus cavities is a matter of squeezing your nose shut through the face mask and forcing air into your eustachian tubes and up into your middle ear and sinuses, thus equalizing the water pressure outside the ear with the air pressure inside the ear. I make it a practice to clear my ears as soon as I drop my head into the water to begin my descent. I do this to keep pressure from building in my ears, but also it prevents the noise of ears clearing at a deeper depth that could be heard by the fish, thus alerting them to my presence.

Body movement burns up oxygen. The more efficient your movements in the water the slower the oxygen will be consumed. The largest muscles in our bodies are the thigh muscles, and they demand the most oxygen. By limiting this heavy muscle activity whenever possible, you can improve your bottom time considerably. So, keep kicking to a minimum and glide whenever possible.

Underwater gliding can be sustained for a remarkable length of time and distance. You have to play with it a little. I generally find that if I level off at neutral buoyancy after a solid surface dive, and then slowly drop a foot or two as my glide begins to falter, I can glide for a considerable distance in currentless water. Of course diving in a current, one can glide the length of a breath-hold, which is as close to the sensation of flight as humans can achieve, and is a highly recommended piece of play when the opportunity presents itself.

Naturally the weight that you are carrying on a belt to neutralize the buoyancy of a wet suit is a factor that strongly influences gliding, and surface diving. By adding or removing lead you can adjust the levels of neutral buoyancy. The idea is to find a comfortable depth that provides the best overall view of the permitting visibility that is within the limits of your breath-hold.

When the need for oxygen signals that the dive is over, ascend quietly, and give a look up when you near the surface to insure that the way is clear. Avoid rushing up to the surface and popping through in a frenzied rush. Round off the dive, blow out the snorkel as previously described, and relax. Don't try and recapture your breath all at once. If that becomes necessary, then you are probably stretching your dives beyond a comfortable limit.

Breath-hold diving presents certain problems that the scuba diver is not confronted with. The most obvious of which is that he must return to the surface invariably at a time when things are getting interesting; perhaps a creature was found or a cave was discovered just as the diver ran out of air and was beginning her ascent.

Often new divers will pop up, look around to reaffirm their location in relation to the shore or some other reference of safety. If they are diving in their comfort zone, there is no need for them to take their eyes from the ocean below. This is another opportunity to exercise the martial art aspects of snorkeling; concentration on what is before them. Because the underwater environment is in constant movement, it becomes difficult to relocate a cave or particular area in the water; so it is doubly important not to break eye-contact with the water beneath you. If you wish to return to a particular area, say a small cave that is hidden in tall sea weed or kelp, create a visual trail from there to a spot that is visible from the surface. Pick out fixed objects such as boulders or outcroppings that are relative to the cave (sea marks is my term for such objects), and stay visually connected with these sea marks until you've recaptured your breath; then follow them back to the entrance of the cave. By diving with this sort of concentration, you will see much more and are more likely to fall into a rhythm of diving that is not unlike the seal or sea lion, moving within the ocean and having broad panoramas of water in which to work.

One of the attractive aspects of snorkeling is that it can be done with a minimum of equipment. If the water is warm, all you need is a mask, snorkel, and a pair of fins. In colder water you'll probably need a wet suit and a weight belt. The face mask should be of low volume for the most efficient use of limited air supply. (The deeper one dives the greater the water pressure on the mask and the more frequently one must equalize that pressure with air blown through the nose to fill the space in the mask.) When purchasing a face mask make sure it fits comfortably and snugly on your face. A leaky mask is the worst kind of distraction in snorkeling; avoid it at all cost. Test the mask for leakage right there in the store by placing it on your face and sucking some air through your nose. If the mask stays on your face by suction alone you can be reasonably sure it won't leak in the water. The "shotgun" type snorkel is well-suited for snorkeling. It's easy to clear and has a large diameter for easy, comfortable breathing.

The type of fins used for snorkeling vary, depending upon the physical characteristics of each individual. Stiff, long-bladed fins are thought to be best for snorkeling because the need for a strong ascent from depth is sometimes required. However, stiff fins can cause leg cramps if your legs have been used to a softer, more flexible fin or you have not used fins at all. You might want to stick with the fins you are now using, and, if you wish to make a change, then make a gradual one, moving to a slightly stiffer fin as your legs are able to handle them. If you buy a set of new fins, make sure they fit comfortably without pinching or cramping your foot. The slightest discomfort can quickly turn to agony after a half hour of solid kicking.

The mechanics of snorkeling, while relatively simple, do require time to perfect. The more you do it the better you will become. Listen to yourself and always endeavor to be as smooth and silent as the inhabitants themselves. Find and sustain a rhythm of your dive, stay alert to the ocean inhabitants, they are the guide by which you can measure your development and skills.

Eventually, perhaps, you will one day enter the underwater world and discover that there is no barrier between you and it, that you are no longer the intruder, but an accepted member of the environment. Once this happens the ocean will never be the same again. You will see it as it is, a silent natural world filled with the most wondrous sights on the planet, that, are best seen when it is not aware of being observed.

c. e.
winter of '84

The Speargun

DEGEI WAS WRAPPED in a tattered, light-weight blanket on the floor of the bure, (Fijian word for sleeping house) when Ba and Ratu appeared at the doorway. Degei rolled over on the soft, burnished, palm frond matting, and opened eyes that were round and innocent like a child's, and blinked long lashes for which, when he was younger, the girls teased him out of envy.

"Ni sa yadra, (good morning)," called Ba cheerfully.

"Bula," replied Degei, rising sleepily to his feet. He shuffled outside to a bucket that was alongside the bure and splashed water on his face and shook himself awake. Unlike Ba and Ratu, who were tall and heavy in the shoulders, Degei was short and wiry, except in the thighs where braided muscles punctuated his every step. He entered an adjoining hut that had waist high walls and was the open kitchen where his wife, Bala, was grinding coconut into mash and his sister Tui was tending an open fire beneath a sheet of iron where rested a black kettle, trembling with boiling water. Degei snatched two pieces of fried cassava root from beneath a clean cloth where it was kept from the flies, and devoured one in a single mouthful. He picked up the unopened nut of a husked coconut and tossed it to Ratu who caught it easily with his free hand. In his other hand he held a thin rusty spear and a pair of plastic goggles that were attached by a ragged piece of cloth. Ba also carried a spear and goggles, and it was these same articles that Degei now dug out of a corner among a rusting harpoon, a fishing net, a broken-handled ax, and a cane knife, which was similar to a machete, but with a smaller blade and which most Fijians did not travel far without. Degei picked up the cane knife and Ratu banged his cane knife against one of the tree limbed support posts of the bure indicating that his knife was enough, and Degei set it back down.

The three walked down to a long beach of white sand and looked out across glassy, turquoise water that beneath the surface held shimmering jewels of white and purple coral. The beauty of the shallows was an unseen thing, and they looked beyond to the open water for a sign of wind or waves on the far-breaking barrier reef. There was no evidence of either.

They came to an old skiff among several pulled high on the beach. It was the skiff of Waqa, and they laid their spears and coconut in the bow and began to drag the boat down to the water. They had not asked Waqa for permission to use the skiff. They simply took it. If Waqa were to come down to the beach later to use his boat for fishing and it was gone, he would not be angry, even if he had made the plan to fish yesterday. For there was no such thing as stealing if you have no intention of keeping the thing you had taken. Waqa would just have to borrow somebody else's boat.

Of the three young men, all in their mid-twenties, it was the youngest, Ba, who rowed the boat out to the barrier reef. Upon reaching the reef they anchored the boat with a stone tied to a line, and then entered the water. A carnation-white reef of coral billowed beneath them, and fish of every aspect and color danced like winged insects about its stone-flowered petals.

The visibility was in excess of a hundred and twenty feet, and though they called it diving, when they glided toward the reef they appeared to be flying in the liquid atmosphere. The goggles that were tied behind their heads with a cloth were of hard plastic and bit painfully into their eye sockets whenever they dove deep. So it was much better to stay shallow and spear the small fish. Though Degei had a fondness for the big coral trout and could not resist the depths, and frequently dove to fifty feet and beyond to look in the caves for a sleeper. The others were content to spear hand-sized fish. If they came across a big one in a cave they would spear it, but they rarely looked deep.

The pencil-thin spears were unbarbed and pointed at one end, and blunted at the other. It was this blunt end that was fitted into a leather piece, much like a sling shot. A single band of rubber was attached to a leather thong that was wrapped around the thumb of the left hand and pulled back with the right hand. The spearshaft was held in the left hand much like a pool cue, and aimed in the same manner. The divers would find their fish from the surface, lift their heads from the water for a final breath, pull back the rubber sling, and descend like stone statues to the depths. So still was their descent that it appeared, from the fish's point of view on the bottom, that they were not moving so much as they were simply getting larger. Fish, which react to sudden movement, would be unaware of the diver until he would release the free spear, usually hitting the fish dead center and breaking its backbone, or striking the eye, hitting the brain. Rarely did they miss a shot, or did the fish fight. Without fins, they would frog-kick their way back to the surface and deposit the fish in the boat. So deftly and silently did they work beneath the sea, that the white tip sharks, which will stir from the peripheries of the reef upon the frantic movements of a wounded fish, or of blood, scarcely made an appearance. And if they did, the divers would ignore them and continue to hunt despite their presence. And never would they forfeit a fish to a shark, even under the most severe circumstances. For once the shark had taken a fish from a diver, it would become bold and compete for every speared fish. On occasion these renegade sharks would have to be hunted down, and many spears would be lost. The Fijians considered the white tip to be their friend, and they did not want to make it an enemy by giving it an easy meal.

Degei discovered a sleeping coral trout in a deep cave. Unhesitatingly he fired the thin spear into the fish, striking its back-bone. Reaching into the cave and with great effort, he pulled the fish free, cutting himself on the coral as he did. The fish was a drab orange in color, and covered with iridescent blue spots. It was heavy in his hand as he kicked powerfully to the surface. Fifteen kilos, thought Degei, as he lifted it into the boat, a good fish.

By late morning the three had speared two dozen fish and headed back to the island of Naitauba, to clean their catch and eat as much of it as they could for lunch and then later for dinner.

They had skewered the small fish through the gills with one of the spears that Ba and Ratu carried at each end, while Degei toted the coral trout over his shoulder. They were met at the bure of Degei by a valagi, a white man. It was unusual to see a valagi on this island so far away from the northern group. He was brought by Seru who had come by boat from Vanua Balavu. Seru said that the valagi, whose name was Robert, was looking for big fish to spear. He had been told of the long reef, far outside, that held the grouper and mackerel that weighed fifty kilos and more. He had brought with him the long blades for his feet, and a speargun that was nearly as tall as a man. It was made of polished wood that gleamed in the sun. It had three big rubbers that fit into a silver spear, and had a deadly point at its tip. It was a speargun of great beauty and power.

Bala and Tui gutted the fish and were preparing to cook them in hot oil. Degei asked Seru to invite the valagi to sit and eat lunch with them. The fish was served whole and the hungry divers were ravenous. They ate everything but the bones. The valagi, they observed, picked at his fish, and left the skin and the head and the eyes and the tail. It was a terrible waste, thought Ratu; the dog would get fat with the valagi around. All the small fish were eaten during the meal, only the coral trout remained, still strung from its gills to the tree.

After they finished their meal Robert was drawn to the coral trout, and though carefully inspecting it, could not find the spear hole on the thirty pound fish. Degei walked over to the fish and lifted up the pectoral fin, and underneath there was a tiny hole where the spear had struck. The flesh was intact indicating no sign of a struggle, and Robert realized that the fish had been killed instantly with the one shot. He nodded, impressed with the feat.

Degei shrugged indifferently.

Robert picked up one of the spears and its odd little leather piece and rubber and attempted to unravel the mystery of its use. Ba came smiling and fixed the leather loop around his thumb, and showed him where to place the shaft and how to pull it back between his fingers. Robert made the attempt, and the spear flew weakly off to the left coming close to Ratu who danced out of the way as the others erupted with laughter. Robert, smiling at himself, tried again. The rubber was difficult to pull back and his arm shook from the tension, which in turn wobbled the spear and the Fijians ran behind him, expecting the worse. The shaft flew but ten feet and skidded along the ground, and Robert shook his head and handed the leather and rubber back to Ba, then lifted his hands in accepted failure.

Robert spoke to Degei through Seru who translated. He said

that he would like to hunt the barrier reef for the big fish, the mackerel, grouper and jack. He would pay for the rental of the boat and a fee to Degei for taking him to the fish. Also he would need a place to sleep. In six days Seru would come back in the boat and pick him up and return him to Vanua Balavus.

Degei was uncertain about the request. Rentals and payment were unnecessary and was perhaps the way of the valagi, but a visitor to Naitauba was always a welcome guest.

Seru left in his boat and Degei escorted the vulagi to the bure of his uncle who had gone to Suva. It was a good bure, one that didn't leak, and it had a soft mat for sleeping. The valagi should be comfortable there. Degei left him and went to his own bure for the afternoon nap.

The valagi, Degei was told upon awakening, had wandered the village, and was down on the beach, collecting shells. Degei stayed in the kitchen and drank tea with Ba and Ratu. They were discussing which reef to take the valagi to tomorrow. The big speargun also had the long line attached, and they reasoned he could spear any fish in the sea; and there would be no worry that the fish would take the spear because it was connected by the line.

"Such a spear could kill a sixty kilo grouper," observed Ratu.

Degei nodded in agreement. "Such a fish would feed everyone in the village."

Ba's eyes grew wide with the realization. "The diver with such a spear would be the best hunter in all Fiji, eh."

That night, around a rough-cut wooden table, Robert ate supper with Degei. Bala and Tui served the men and would eat after they had finished. They cooked a special meal for the valagi of breadfruit, cassava, and belle with coconut milk, and a large piece of the coral trout that was covered with shredded coconut and sprinkled with minced pepper. It was delicious. The valagi seemed to enjoy the meal, and this pleased the women who had prepared it over the single open flame.

In the morning Degei and Ratu rowed the valagi out to the reef. He wore a suit of rubber, and had a fine window for his face and a tube for breathing, and the long blades for his feet, and of course the beautiful wooden speargun with the three rubbers.

The valagi was a good diver. He went deep and stayed down a long time. When he speared a fish though, his shot was bad, and the fish fought and ran for the coral and brought the white tips. He had speared a grouper of thirty kilos and it had gone into a cave and he could not pull it out. The sharks came and circled the cave, smelling the blood, and the valagi kicked for the surface and would not dive for the fish, not even to get back the spear that was in it. From the surface he tried to pull the fish out with the line, but that was foolish, for the fish had opened its gills and wedged itself inside. The cave was sixty feet deep and Degei inhaled his breath and frog-kicked his way to the cave, pushing away sharks as they neared him and hitting one on the nose with his fist. He peered inside the cave and found the fish wedged deep inside the coral. He reached in as far as he could and pulled on the spear until he could touch the fish and then gently closed its gills and began to pull it out. Before it came free however, it reopened its gills and Degei had to let it go for he was out of breath, and kick his way back to the surface.

Impressed, Robert nodded his head in approval and patted Degei on the shoulder when he was recovering his breath on the surface. When he looked up, the valagi was holding the blades for the feet and handed them to him.

Like all Fijians, Degei had oversized feet, and though he had not the rubber sock the valagi wore, the blades fit his feet when the strap was pulled tight.

He inhaled a breath and bent into the water, and when the blades had cleared the surface he began to kick. The water ran by his ears like a strong wind, and the top of the reef seemed to leap from the depths. He was at the cave in an instant. It was the most astounding thing that had ever happened to him in the water. He was as fast as a fish with the blades, and his breath was still fresh in his chest. He pulled the fish from the cave with ease, pushed a shark away then carried the sixty pound fish up to the surface with ease. Light as a sea bird he soared to the rippling sea/sky. He was still holding his breath when he reached the surface and was putting the fish in the boat because there was so much of it left. The valagi was sitting in the boat, and when Degei began to take off the blades to return them, he waved him away. Degei took his own spear and made another dive, this time in the deep water over the edge of the reef. Ratu watched him descend to the reef, then beyond down past a hundred feet near the bottom. Ratu saw the spear release and Degei turn and head for the surface. He was carrying a fish, another coral trout of fifteen kilos, the fish was dead and had no fight like the valagi's. When he brought it to the boat the valagi took it and inspected for the spear hole finding it to be in the same place as the one yesterday. He shook his head in near disbelief and glanced admiringly at Degei, who, while he still wore the blades, was pre-occupied with the depths, and anxious to spear another coral trout. Which he did on the next dive in the same manner.

That night they drank kava in a circle around a fire. The valagi was with them, and though he could not speak Fijian, was pleased to be included.

"You should have seen Degei with the blades on his feet," said Ratu to Bala. "He dove beyond the top of the reef to the bottom where the grouper live. It was something to see."

"Did you move quickly?" asked Bala to Degei.

"I was like a dolphin. I could have gone deeper, my breath was full. To swim at such a speed is most amazing. The man who wears those blades would be the best diver in all of Fiji. There would be no reef too deep for him to dive. He could hunt the coral trout and bring up four or five a day."

"What about the grouper, could he hunt the grouper too?" asked Bala.

"The grouper are too big for our spears. There is too much of them for the spear to push through and then break the backbone which is as big as the bones of a man. No, our spears are too small. I saw many that were bigger than myself, and unafraid. They looked at me and wondered what a man was doing so deep in their water."

Everyone laughed at the thoughts of the grouper.

The effect of the kava had the valagi's mouth slacking and his shoulders sagged. The Fijians gestured and smiled at him, but he was unaware and didn't look up from the fire.

The night soon became old, and it was time to eat.

The valagi was helped to his feet, but did not wish to eat. Instead he was lead to his bure where he dreamed narcotic dreams and did not awake until late the next morning. Empty in the mind and hollow in the eye, he could not entreat the will to dive from his deadened body. He ate fried cassava and rice and drank lemon grass tea, but it didn't improve his condition as the Fijians had promised.

They did not go diving that day. Nor did the valagi drink kava that night. He politely waved it off, to the understanding of all in the group.

The following morning the valagi went out in the boat and they dove the barrier reef again. Even with his blades the valagi could not dive deep enough to spear the grouper that were drifting like great logs at the very bottom of the reef. He did spear a mackerel that was a free swimmer, and it fought with fury and brought the sharks again. But this time he held tightly to the line and kicked hard with the blades and kept the fish from diving into the coral. He was pleased with the fish; it was over thirty kilos, and when they came ashore in the afternoon, he showed Degei how to hold the black box that made the picture. After that day the valagi wished only to spear the free swimmers, the mackerel and the jack. The next day Degei showed him another reef where the mackerel came with frequency, and he speared three. When he was done and sitting in the boat, he handed the face glass with the tube to Degei, and gestured that he put it on and try it in the water.

Degei floated face down in the water. The face glass was surrounded by softness and did not dig into the bone of the eye as the plastic goggles. Also he could see from side to side and up and down without turning his head. But it was the tube that made the dive easy. Such a simple thing. He did not have to hold his breath when looking for fish from the surface, and when he inhaled the big breath for the dive he was relaxed and it went deep into his chest. Even without the blades on his feet he was able to dive to sixty-five feet with the fresh air in his chest. He had watched the valagi blow out the water from the tube when he returned to the surface, and only once did he swallow water when he began to breathe again when there was still water in the tube. The tube had removed the toil from the dive, and Degei believed that in such comfort he could dive all day and never be in need of rest.

On the last day the valagi speared a very large jack, over seventy kilos. He was very pleased with this fish and had Degei take many pictures of him with the fish. When Seru came to fetch the valagi the next morning, Degei was told that the jack was a world record and that was why the valagi was so pleased. Degei, Ratu and Ba knew nothing of world records, they had seen fish larger than that, and with the blades and the tube, and the powerful speargun, any fish in the sea was possible. Even if the hunter was such a terrible shot as the valagi seemed to be.

When the valagi was about to leave on Seru's boat he did a truly generous thing; he presented to Degei the blades for his feet, the face glass with the tube, and lastly handed him the speargun. It was a gift for a chief and Degei received it with humility.

The next morning Ba and Ratu and Degei were in the borrowed skiff of Waqa rowing out to the barrier reef as the sun ignited the high clouds turning their feathered tips to delicate, pale rainbows.

With ceremonial precision Degei dressed into the diving gear. When he was in the water he cocked the three rubbers on the gun that was now without the long line, and floated above the reef inhaling easy breaths as one who was confidently aware of the extent of power that was at his command. After a final breath he bent into the water and descended into the crystalline water. The blades propelled him to the sand beneath the reef in a hundred and twenty feet of water. He laid on a large boulder as the circling grouper moved closer to inspect the intruder. Lining up on one that was seventy kilos, he pulled the trigger and the spear released like a bolt of lightening. It entered the fish exactly where he had aimed and broke the fish's backbone. He drifted over to the fish and put a hand in its gill and began the long haul up the surface.

Ba and Ratu had watched Degei spear the fish, and now he was bringing it up. It was a very long way to carry a seventy kilo fish. His heavily muscled thighs strained against the water, and the blades were bent nearly double from the stress. Already he had been down over two minutes, and still he had to swim another fifty feet.

He burst through the surface and blew out an explosive breath, but almost immediately his breathing returned to normal. He swam the fish to the boat, but Ba without Ratu's help, could not heft the fish into the boat. Together they lifted it over the gunwales, and let it lay where it fell.

"This is the biggest fish ever speared by a village man," declared Ba. "Maybe it is the biggest fish ever speared by a Fiji man, eh."

"This fish will feed everyone in the village for two days," announced Ratu. "There will be a celebration tonight. Kava will be drunk by the gallons."

Degei nodded, smiling. While he was a good diver, he knew that it was the blades, the tube, and the speargun that had made it possible for him to land the fish. There were others in the village who could have done the same. Still, it was a mighty fish, and he was pleased to have brought it out of the ocean, and was honored to feed the village.

That night there was indeed a celebration. At the kava circle of the elders, chief Sigatoka acknowledged the skill of Degei to bring up such a fish, and they also gave thanks to the Sea God for bestowing the village with such a gift. The kava was drunk until heads rested on chests and men toppled over from their sitting positions. They could so indulge because tomorrow and the day after there would be no need to fish, and one could sleep all day without worry that there would be nothing to eat.

In two days the village had consumed the grouper and enough kava to run a well dry. On the morning of the third day Degei left with Ba and Ratu in the skiff to find another grouper. All the boats in the village were waiting for him and were filled to the gunnels with men and woman intent on following Degei out to the barrier reef to watch him spear another fish. If he did, there would be no need for them to work with the spear or the fishing line for another two days. Even the women who usually dive for the clams and shells would have no need to enter the water. Everyone was waiting to see what Degei would do with the speargun.

All the men and woman with goggles got into the water as Degei cocked the speargun. They watched him dive with the blades and descend past the coral reef and into the sand at the bottom, that could have been the surface of the moon for its accessibility to the rest. They heard the release of the spear and saw the fish quiver in its death throes, and then Aprosa began the difficult climb up from the depths. As he came, the fish grew larger and larger and when he reached the top everyone let out a cheer; for this fish appeared larger than the last. And it took two men to haul it into a boat. Everyone rowed and paddled back to the village, laughing and grinning in anticipation of the evening that was destined for wonderful drunkenness again.

Weeks and then months passed and Degei continued to bring fish to the village as it was needed. His name circled the islands, everyone on Vanua Balavu and Mago, and as far away as Koro, Lakeba and Qamea, had heard about the young Fijian man who was spearing a single fish that could feed a village for two days.

One afternoon Degei was called to the bure of Chief Sigatoka. The old chief was grave, and there was concern etched on his face. He beckoned Degei to sit and told him what a fine diver he was, and that he had brought honor to the village, and that the other villages on the other islands would remember them both with talk and stories. But it was his responsibility as chief to always do what was best for the village. The village came before a man or a woman or even a chief.

Sigatoka paused. "There is harm being brought to this village because there is no need for the others to fish or spearfish. All that is left is work in the garden and the digging for roots in the bush. It is not enough. The people believe they are happy with less work, but they are not. They are drinking kava every night trying to forget their uselessness. Something must be done."

Degei was confused. He had no thoughts that such were the problems of the village. "Everyone seems happy that there is always an abundance of fish," he said.

"It only appears that way," explained Sigatoka. "Things often are not what they appear, eh."

This was so, and Degei nodded in agreement. "What is it that you wish me to do?" he asked

Sigatoka's mouth was grim, and the air whistled from his nose in a long sigh.

"You must bury the speargun somewhere in the sea where it will never be found. If there comes a time, such as a hurricane that might destroy all our boats, and we have nothing to eat, then we might need the speargun again. But for now you must dive deep with the blades to a place no one can reach and bury the speargun."

Chief Sigatoka was wise in ways Degei did not understand. That was why he was chief. If it was best for the village to bury the speargun, then he would do so without question.

The following morning, before the sun had thoughts of firing the sky into day, Degei rowed a skiff alone to the barrier reef. When the sun rose above the horizon, and lit the undersea world enough to see, he slid into the water and descended to the deepest section of the reef at a hundred and forty feet. There were grouper already moving when he came, and they watched him slip the gun into a small cave, and push it deep inside and then ascend. Without the weight of the fish to hold him back he lifted like a bird and soared to the lighted ceiling, weightless and free of burden.

He climbed into the boat and rowed back toward the islands. The rising sun dried his skin. He would tell Ba and Ratu that he had mis-placed a shot and the grouper had swum away so strongly that it had pulled the speargun from his hand and then disappeared around the north end of the reef. The opposite end that he had buried the spear. He knew that the village would be looking for the fish and the speargun, and that anyone who found it would claim it for their own.

The grouper of course was never found, nor was the speargun.

Several years later Degei checked the cave to see if it was still there, but the sea had covered it with its growth and frozen it with coral, and never again did he look inside the cave.

Around the kava circle at night, the village elders spoke often of the speargun, and the legend of it was carried on in story over the years. Every year several of the young boys would borrow a skiff and spend a few weeks looking for the speargun. Eventually they would give up the search, but the following year another set of boys would take it up, all hoping to find the speargun and become a part of its legend as the greatest spearfisherman in all of Fiji.

Stalking

S TALKING IN THE GENERAL SENSE of the term cannot quite apply to underwater hunting as it does to other, land-bound forms of hunting. Webster's dictionary defines stalk as: to pursue quarry or prey stealthily. Unfortunately, the pursuit of fish is limited to underwater visibility, which is measured in feet, not yards or miles. In other words, once the fish splits, it's gone, no trail, no scent, out of sight, nothing. Thus the stalking of fish underwater must take place first in the mind. By that I mean the hunter must understand all he can about the fish he is stalking: eating habits, routes, water temperature and thermocline inclinations, food sources, terrain preferences, responses to sound, movement, and human intrusion. All this so that the hunter might successfully intersect the fish within the confines of its territory under the restrictions of limited visibility.

I can recall only one instance in thirty five years where I actually stalked a fish, a white sea bass, as Webster would define stalk. I suspect this one exception would underscore the rule of the impossibility of an extended underwater stalk.

I was on Eagle Reef at Catalina Island on one of those overcast mornings in June about an hour after dawn. The seas were slick as marble, and the water skiers were running full blast up and down the island about a hundred yards off the reef. The visibility was exceptional, the clearest I had seen it that summer, maybe sixty feet. I spotted the white sea bass from the surface, inhaled a soft breath, no noise; pulled out my snorkel, no bubbles; jack-knifed down, no kicking, to twenty-five feet and glided toward the fish which weighed about forty pounds. It never saw or heard me. However, to get within range, I had to ease through a school of bait that, when I drew near, exploded into silent, silver chards, spooking the white from where it lay stationary between two kelp stalks. It still hadn't seen me and drifted out and away from the reef into deep water. Out of breath, I lifted up to the surface, never breaking visual contact with the fish. When I reached the top, the white was at the very limit of visibility, and rapidly becoming a lighter shade of blue against the blue background of the water. Kicking ever so gently so as not to further spook the fish, but enough to keep in visual contact, I followed it. The white had left the reef and was swimming in mid-water towards the island a mile away. If I were to take my eyes from the fish for an instant, or even blink, the shade of blue I was stalking would disappear into the background and be lost. To complicate matters I was swimming directly across the paths of the water skiers. (Moving boat traffic is the single greatest hazard to free-dive spearfishermen. Those in the boats can scarcely see the low, nearly invisible profile of the hunter in the water. There isn't a blue water hunter around that hasn't had a close shave (pun intended) with a powerboat. I'm surprised more hunters aren't run over and seriously injured. I couldn't look up, for fear of losing the fish, and the whine of hard-driving props seemed to be coming from every direction. The fish continued to swim for another hundred yards and then stopped and hovered in the open water fifty feet from the surface. When I caught up to it, I dove from directly above, and put a shaft into it. Working quickly, I was able to get the fish to my hand before regaining the surface. Moments after surfacing, a boat flew by no more than ten feet away, followed by the water skier who turned and looked aghast at what had to be an astonishing sight; a man who, out in the middle of open water, suddenly materialized from beneath the boat lifting a great silver fish that was whipping around in a fine frenzy. No doubt that particular stalk was as amazing to me as my appearance was to the water skier.

So, bearing in mind that stalking fish is first a matter of understanding the behavior of the fish being hunted, as well as being thoroughly familiar with the area of water you might be working, (understanding that areas of water often differ greatly from mile to mile along a coast line), I can offer only pieces of the puzzle of underwater stalking that might be of value.

There are almost as many different techniques of stalking as there are species of fish. To cover them all would require a full-length book. The most common and perhaps most interesting technique is the open-water stalk for large, pelagic fish. (Naturally with this type of fish the hunter would need the proper rigging, because these fish are generally among the most powerful that swim in the oceans.)

I can think of no other analogy for hunting pelagic fish in open water than that of learning to catch a fly ball. It appears so easy when you see it done by professional ball players, yet from the time the ball is hit to the time it is caught, there are dozens of calculations and adjustments that the outfielder must make. None of which are consciously thought out. The ball player doesn't tell himself, "Well now, the ball is accelerating at one hundred and three miles an hour on a trajectory of twenty-six and a half degrees and thus should, allowing for deceleration and moisture in the air, fall approximately nineteen yards from where I now stand. I have to take seven steps to my right and fourteen steps back, and now I have to adjust for the wind that is blowing in from left-center field and go in three steps, and now I have to run at three-quarter speed, and now I have to lengthen my stride and now I have to extend my arm over my head and now I have to... If he had thought about any one of those responses he would have missed the ball.

So it is with spearing open water fish the likes of yellowtail, jack, wahoo, tuna, dorado, etc. There are probably as many calculations involved with stalking an open water fish as there are to catching a fly ball, and all of them must be made instinctively. How do you do it? Same way you learn to catch a fly ball, you gotta do it a lot of times, and make a lot of mistakes before you get it down. And then you still have to be accurate with the shot. And that's a whole other ball game.

I'll try and break down a single stalk on say a yellowtail as I did with the fly ball. But I must advise you in advance that none of it will do any good at the time you're making the stalk. Perhaps later, after you've blown the fish, you can break it down and say, oh yeah, I shouldn't have turned so quickly, or something equally as inconsequential. Anyway here goes.

Let's assume for the moment that all conditions are perfect; (a rarity to begin with, but let's not complicate this anymore than necessary), there is no current, the water is clear and the fish aren't unduly spooky. From the surface you spot the yellowtail moving on the outside from your left to right. (The ball is hit.) You make an unhurried drop facing the exact direction the fish is swimming so that your dive is actually paralleling it. You never want to head for the fish directly, for that is translated into an aggressive act that will almost always spook the fish into flight. Observe the fish from your peripheries, if at all. Level off at the same depth the fish is swimming. Wait motionless with gun extended, ready to shoot, body laid out directly behind the gun to line up the shot. If you're lucky, the curiosity of the fish will have it swing in an arc in front of you and come within range without you ever having to adjust the shot. Easy fly ball they call it, a can of corn, for baseball aficionados.

However, most of the time the fish swings wide, and you have to lure it, via its curiosity, toward you by holding up your free hand and waving it or wiggling your fingers. (At this point of course it's all right to be facing it, as long as you're not swimming toward it.) The fish could come to your right or left, high or low. Without any quick or jerky movements track the fish with the gun, making adjustments dictated by the movements of the fish; this while waving your hand, and, perhaps, moving imperceptively forward a foot or two just before you take the shot. This will level out the shot, and add impetus to the flight of the spear. But maybe the fish isn't so cooperative. Maybe it swings wide to the right, and wants to circle. In which case you don't track it with the speargun or maybe you do, it depends on the skittishness of the fish. Maybe it would be better to slowly swing back in the opposite direction and meet it off your left shoulder as it completes the circle. Now maybe you're beginning to sink or rise and you have to kick to compensate, and that might be spooking the fish, and it won't come into range. Or you're running out of breath while the fish is creeping into range a foot at a time with each pass, which is not uncommon. What do you do? (Take a wild shot and hope you get it? No, don't take a wild shot on hope. Take the shot that is certain. It's a terrible thing to lose a speared fish.) Maybe you tough out the breath-hold, or maybe you rise for a breath, or maybe, as some have done, you begin to swim away on your back with the gun trailing between your legs in hope that the fish might follow, which they have been known to do.

Lots of maybes in the craft of stalking a fish. One simply can't account for all the variables. There are just too many possibilities to have a hard and fast formula. No two stalks are ever alike because the fish will never respond in exactly the same way, nor will the conditions be exactly the same, nor will your position to the fish ever be exactly the same. When you're operating in an environment that permits you to move up and down, side to side, backward and forward, it adds an unfamiliar dimension, like trying to catch a fly ball while hovering twenty feet above the ground. Different ball game.

As I said, you gotta play the game a lot before you're able to get a real feel for it. When you have internalized it, it becomes this wonderful skill that is difficult to describe, like trying to describe every decision that incorporates catching a fly ball. But once it's inside of you, it's something you'll never forget, not entirely. There is a sharp edge to hunting fish that is achieved by doing it all the time. If you take time off, the edge can be dulled. But the more you stalk, the quicker the edge will be regained. Perhaps one day the edge will be sharpened after a single dive, because you've been doing it for so long that it becomes no more than a matter of wetting the surface of your skin with sea water for all the underwater knowledge to come flooding back with the clarity of one who has never been away.

The greatest pleasure I have in spearfishing is in the stalk. The least of which has been the open water stalk as I have described above. Though there is enormous satisfaction in making all the right moves, knowing that one small mistake would have blown the fish. Yet one does not have to stalk big, pelagic fish to experience all the elements of a stalk that are so invigorating. One of the finest hunters I know, big fish or small, thoroughly enjoys hunting for seven to ten pound calico bass in the kelp beds along the California Coast. A hunter's stalking skills are severely tested with this fish. Calico bass have keen eyesight and are hypersensitive to noise and movement. Their response to a hunter's mistake is immediate, and thus will teach him everything he needs to know about stalking in the kelp.

Stalking in kelp is like hunting in a forest of trees. There is great appeal in the stalk when you have to be conscious of every move and of every sound because there might be a fish around the next kelp stalk. In fact if you don't approach the stalk in this fashion, there will never be a fish around the next kelp stalk. They would have heard you coming and simply disappeared. "There are no fish in this kelp bed," the careless stalker will lament. When in fact he has spooked them while bouncing through the bed. When the stalk is smooth and noiseless, there is always action in the kelp bed. It is one of the best places to work on descents, breath-holds, and developing the vision to properly read the lay of the bed. It has been said that if a hunter can successfully hunt calico, he can hunt anything.

While I've enjoyed hunting for calico, I have always been drawn to the big fish. I have gone many a day and week without ever pulling the trigger in pursuit of big fish. I suspect that it is the power of the fish on the line that is so irresistible. There is something wonderfully primal about that force.Until the last few thousand years, man had speared, roped, and stoned his prey until finally he had to haul it down on arm strength alone, ultimately reaching the point where it was his strength pitted against that of the animal. So for man to be dragged about by the power of an animal is something with which our ancient genes are familiar. For me, it reawakens the core of my biological function and in a very primal way carries me to a place where I am able to abide in perfect harmony with the ebb and flow of the natural world beneath the sea.

While I have had my share of big fish stalks, the ones that seem to stand out in memory are not the stalks where I used a big gun. They were stalks where I landed a big fish, using a small gun and a large measure of intuition. The intuitive sense of hunting can't be taught or conveyed in how-to books. It must be learned out there in the water, time after time after time until one has internalized every situation and knows every move and counter move until it is understood without thought.

While living in Fiji and hunting for fish as a source of food every other day for six months, this intuitive sense asserted its influence. When I first arrived on the island of Qamea and began diving the waters around my beach for food, I came across a silver fish with a white spot on its back that weighed between eighteen and twenty five pounds. It was a species of snapper that the Fijians promised was the most delicious eating in Fiji. There were maybe half a dozen of these fish on the two hundred yards of reefs that fingered out into water with drop-offs that ranged from fifty to well over a hundred feet, and they were far and away the spookiest fish in the area. The snapper liked the warm shallow water on top of the reefs that were often just eight feet below the surface. The speargun I was using was four feet long with two bands of rubber and a one wrap shooting line that permitted the spear to go no more than six feet past the end of the muzzle. If I were to spear the fish, I had to be very close. Oddly, whenever I was taking pictures these same fish would come to within five feet of me, but when I had the gun they would watch me from thirty feet away. A usual ploy of mine was to dive down, using the reef for cover, and swim as far as I could, paralleling the reef, then come up slow with gun extended hoping to catch the fish sunning. But everytime I came up the fish would be gone, usually hanging above the reef behind me, observing my every move. Sometimes I would take a breath-hold and dive to the top of the reef in eight feet of water and wait, unmoving. They would often come to inspect me from behind, and if I moved the gun at all they would disappear over the edge of the reef. After spending entire mornings stalking the fish, I'd eventually give up and seek out other fish, for I was hunting for food, and going hungry will always prevail over the most enticing stalk.

Months passed and I became proficient on the reef. I was diving deep and extending my breath-hold to new limits, and still had not come close to even pulling the trigger on a spotted snapper. Every hunting day I would devote at least an hour to the snapper. It was becoming an obsession. The fish knew me as well as I knew them, and as time wore on, unless one of them made a crucial mistake, which they never did, I would never taste the finest fish in Fiji.

One morning in the fifth month I was stalking a particular snapper. It was a game now. I knew it as a game, and it must have been a game for the snapper. When I would make a dive, it would always move below, or above the reef, and out of sight. I would make my move then come up and it would be gone, but I had never seen it move until this one day. The fish was hanging on the far edge, and I was on the near edge of the same reef, maybe thirty feet away. I dove and swam to the end of the reef where a gully of open water separated the reef from another high reef that ran perpendicular to it. I peeked around the corner and saw the fish, seventy feet away, dart over the gully and disappear over the edge of the high reef across from where I lay. I then crossed the twenty feet of open water and slipped into a slice of the reef on the other side and held the gun pointing almost straight up to the surface. I was completely hidden except for the gun. The snapper would have to come to this exact place if I were to have a shot. It came directly to the spot and edged over the slice that was hiding me, the spear not two feet away from it. It was as if I had actually gotten into the mind of the fish, or had internalized its patterns of behavior to such a degree that finally I knew precisely where it would appear. Anywhere else, five feet one way or the other and I would never had been able to spear it.

I have in these last ten years placed myself in the position where I have had to stalk for my food to survive, for at least half of those years. Under those conditions a feeling of connectedness with the fish and the environment has been constant. Stalking has nothing to do with the killing. There comes the same feeling when I am stalking fish for photographs and instinctively know how the fish will behave and exactly where it will appear. Later, when I recall that feeling of connectedness, or oneness, I realize that I had no idea of it at the time. If I did, it would no doubt dissolve and I would become the observer, the civilized man again, disconnected and disenfranchised from the source of himself.

The stalk is my meditation, the instrument whereby I am able to lose my civilized self, and become one with all that surrounds me. The Carlos that the world of man knows disappears, and the true essence of him that has no name operates as comfortably as a creature of the wilderness. I am convinced that in those moments I experience the truest freedom I will ever know.

c. e.
summer of '91

The Education of Jubal Freemountain

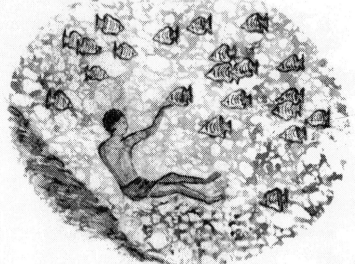

ON AN UNUSUALLY BALMY BAHAMIAN morning in February, as the sun ignited the horizon casting its golden light across the tin roof tops of Cherokee Sound, thirty-five kilometers south of Marsh Harbour on Great Abaco island, a hundred-fifty kilometers north of Nassau, Wallace Freemountain and his wife Ruby, gave birth to a baby boy whom they named Jubal. Ruby, who was a large woman before she was with child, now neared three-hundred pounds. To soothe the pain of the contractions, which had begun near midnight, she had Wallace fetch sea water which he heated over a fire and then poured into an old porcelain tub that had been brought over nearly two centuries ago by British Loyalists. Wallace had found the tub near the old road to Marsh Harbour where it had been used as a stock tank before the road was built so that logs could be easily transported from the forests to the mill in Snake city. He had dragged the tub home and cleaned it up, and it became the centerpiece of their three-room dwelling. Though the home had not seen a coat of paint in nearly eighteen years, it was sturdily constructed from century-old planks of a ship that had run aground when the citizens of Hope Town had darkened the lighthouse to lead forlorn ships astray. Not an unusual occurrence in that part of the ocean where piracy in the 17th century was perfectly legal. "Wrecking", the quaint euphemism among Bahamians, was common trade. The general belief was that ships of the sea were fair game to any and all who were bold enough to take them. On the occasions that a rumrunner would run aground when the light house was darkened, the whole of Great Abaco island would profit from its deception. These days one had to buy his own rum, and during the long labor of Ruby Freemountain, Wallace would liked to have had more than the half bottle that was at his side.

When the time came for Ruby to give birth, she had not the strength to lift herself from the tub, and she found no help in Wallace, who, during the course of the night, had lost much of his coordination. So she gave birth where she sat. The baby was her fifth and it slid easily from between her legs into the warm salt water that was not unlike the liquid warmth of the womb. There were no bright lights of a hospital to pierce the baby's eyes that had only known darkness, and there were no foreign hands to lift and thump him into life. Nor were there any cool instruments to harshly probe his air passages, or slice at his genitals. He lay peacefully in the warm water, his umbilical cord still intact, and in no real hurry to breathe his first breath. The Freemountains marveled at their baby boy who appeared to be smiling under the water. When finally they lifted him to the air, he opened his eyes and inhaled his first breath with nary a whimper on that February morning in the year 1961.

The Freemountain house was a stones throw from the shoreline of Cherokee Sound. It was from there that his father left daily in his skiff to fish the cays for grouper, hogfish, snapper and the occasional jack. In the evening he would sell the fish at the store where a dozen cats marked in yellows and whites always lounged. Whatever he could not sell to the store keeper, he brought home for supper.

Each morning Jubal would be carried by his mother down to the boats drawn up on the sand, and wave good-bye to his father. Then Ruby would set him free in the sand, and like a new-born turtle who instinctively knows its home is not in the sand from which it was born, he would crawl toward the water. As much as she tried, Ruby Freemountain could not keep her son out of the calm, protected, waters of Cherokee Sound. Jubal, she observed, was very much like the island of Great Abaco, (which was more than a third marshland along the western coast), difficult to judge where the water ended and the land began. Before Jubal was two years old, he was completely submerging himself beneath the water with eyes wide, gliding with easy strokes until out of breath. Then he would relax and gently rise to the surface, roll to his back, and breathe unhurried breaths. While other mothers watched carefully over their babies and young ones, Ruby was quite content to recline on the beach beneath the coconut trees and visit with neighbors, her great weight discouraging the relentless chase required to keep up with her energetic son. This permitted Jubal to freely explore the shallows in his own fashion.

Jubal's favorite pastime was to lay beneath the surface of the water and let the gentle surge rock him as if he were back in his mother's womb. It was in these moments of detachment that he began to hear a particular sound that was unlike the usual sounds of the sea. It began at the far edge of the other sounds, beyond the stirring of the sand and the roll of the wave as it folded into itself on the surface. The sound seemed to come from the depth of the sea, and he could not listen for it because it played more in his abdomen than in his ear. It soothed him and would make him forget his body and his breath. One day, after he had left the sea and was warming on the hot sand of the beach, he realized that the sound had traveled into the deep places of himself, for there was a tingling high in his stomach. When he closed his eyes strange and beautiful images appeared that he thought he dreamed.

Daily he would wait for the sound. He never knew how long he waited, though it would seem like a very long time between breaths. Often mothers who were watching over their own children playing in the shallows would see Jubal laying there beneath the water, unmoving, for minutes at a time. Though they knew him well, for they all called him "the water baby," there were occasions when one would rush up to snatch him from the water, fearing that he had drowned. He would always turn and smile sleepy eyed at the woman, and the other mothers on shore would laugh, themselves having been victim at one time or another of Jubal's "water sleeps," as they called them.

With each passing year Jubal ventured further and further from shore. By the time he was four he had followed the sound around the point and was fortunate to have been found by a passing fishing boat before the currents could sweep him away. Everyone in Cherokee Sound had heard of the incident, and all were concerned for the safety of the boy, except Wallace and Ruby. They knew that Jubal was of the sea as a bird was of the sky, but because he was becoming an embarassment to their parenthood, it was decided that Wallace should take him in the skiff on his daily fishing trips.

Wallace worked the reefs from Hole in the Wall to Lynyard Cay. At first he tried to teach Jubal the craft of fishing with the line, "hand lining." But Jubal's interest was beneath the surface and he slipped overboard at every opportunity. After several weeks of reprimand and punishment, with no change in his behavior, Wallace surrendered to the will of his son and allowed Jubal to dive the reefs under the pretense that he dislodge any fish hooks that might become caught in the rocks and coral.

The reefs revealed a new world to Jubal. Without face mask or snorkel, he would drift down to the top of a shallow reef and hold on to rocks or branches of sea trees that grew in miniature forests to the sand. Multi-colored fish, like exotic butterflies, would flutter before his extended hand, and swim unafraid about his head. When he moved, it was with deliberation and ease, and the fish behaved as if he were one of them. Through his naked eye the ocean was vague and fuzzy, and after a time it became Jubal's habit to close his eyes and float weightless in neutral buoyancy and wait to be filled with the sound that came beyond the other ocean sounds. Soon the messages of the sea began to be understood with a clarity he had never known before. He became aware of the subtle upswell that wafted in from the deep water; the change and direction of the tide; the ripple and sound that distinguished the sandy bottom from the rocky bottom, and though they lay unseen, where the deep reefs were hidden. The ocean spoke its language, and it was received through Jubal's skin and belly and was understood.

It was with a mix of awe and delight that Wallace watched his son move so gracefully beneath the sea. His brown body, sleek as a spear, wove effortlessly among the Banzai forests of the sea trees, as if breath and the world of air was a thing removed and forgotten.

"If I dint know bedda," said Wallace to Ruby one evening, "I tink dat boy's fadder be a Sea Obeah. He do tings in da wadda no man eva do."

Among the multitudes of clicks and snaps that the underwater world imparts, Jubal began to detect within that chorus of sound the faint grinding of lobster mandibles. And, descending upon the lobster's hidden den, would gently feel his way down the antenna to the base of the horn and ease it from its hiding place, and bring it to the boat. He could single out the clicking of the ghost shrimp, and the scrape of the parrot fish gnawing on coral. Soon he was distinguishing the cracking tail of the grouper from that of the hogfish. And while able to separate the different sounds, he could also know precisely from which direction they came. Soon he was guiding Wallace to new reefs that had never been fished, and directing his father's hook to the entrance of caves that held the big grouper.

After a time, the sea began to whisper the whereabouts of the silent conch, and then to the empty shells stacked beneath the lair of the octopus. He knew, without seeing, when the eels would come, and did not jump or swim away from them. Instead he would break off a large front leg of the lobster and feed it to the eels, stroking their rubbery skin as they slid around him.

Wallace's boat began to overflow with fish. In the evenings the Freemountain's table was filled with fresh vegetables, bread and bottles of beer. The other fishermen from Cherokee Sound believed that Jubal had brought luck to the boat, but Wallace knew otherwise.

On Jubal's seventh birthday, Wallace gave him a dive mask, snorkel, and a pair of used swim fins. The face mask was Jubal's final key that opened the grand door to the ocean universe. Before him unfolded a world of overwhelming beauty. He now could actually see the power that he had long felt. Yet with all the magnificent colors of the fish, and the breath-taking sculpture in the landscape of the reefs, and the way the light fell upon it all, the messages he received through his skin did not abate in the least. Now, with the swim fins, he could follow those messages to the depths. Depth was not perceived as an obstacle. He accepted a dive to depth as a landlubber might accept a stroll to the corner market. The plummet to sixty feet was effortless, and wherever he needed to go, he went.

In Jubal's ninth year, Wallace made him a sling spear out of a six-inch piece of drilled-out broomstick through which was slid an old umbrella stay that was to become the spear shaft. At one end of the broomstick a loop of surgical tubing was fastened from where the five foot spear was drawn and released, similar to a bow and arrow. Almost immediately Jubal became uncannily accurate with the spear.

He would spot a fish from the surface, then take a breath and pull back on the rubber of the sling and fall, stone still, to the depths. In the glycerine water with the visibility in excess of a hundred feet, the fish, interpreting danger in movement, would perceive no more than an object in their sky that appeared to grow in size. Then, when Jubal was within a foot of the fish, he would release the spear, more often than not striking the backbone, killing the fish instantly. Though most fish he speared were no more than five to ten pounds, he did spear larger fish which would bolt off and out of sight taking the spear with them. And he would have to track them down by listening for their movements. The fish would always seek the concealed cave among the many that honeycombed the reef, and Jubal would always find it and bring it to the surface.

Jubal was bringing great quantities of fish to the boat, and in a short time was doubling his father's take.

One evening, Wallace's skiff, overloaded with fish, swamped and nearly sank from seas that had risen with the afternoon wind. It was a frightful moment; for it represented all that Wallace possessed. After the incident he began to dream dreams of he and Jubal bringing in boatloads of fish everyday. He envisioned a larger boat that would handle the load and take them across the Northeast Providence channel to Eleuthera and the reefs en route. As he was building the boat in his mind, one with perhaps a cabin to protect from the wind and sea, there came the news from Ruby that the authorities had come looking for Jubal. They wanted to know why he was not attending school with other children his age.

Fearing that Jubal might be deprived of an education she and her children never had, as well as the meddling and possible sharp rebuke from the authorities, Ruby Freemountain insisted her son be sent to school.

"Dis chile gon to hab sompin we neber hab. He gon to hab a chance to mek his wey in da worl'. We cain gib him much, but we cain gib him dat." Wallace Freemountain knew that Jubal had a wisdom of the sea that was unlike anything he had ever seen. With such a knowledge a man needed nothing else to survive. But maybe in this new world, that particular wisdom had no meaning. Maybe it was better that he got this new knowledge for the new world. This he told himself as a father who would sacrifice a dream of a new boat for the future of his son.

The school house was once a Loyalist home, with white-washed boards, trimmed in red, and peaked roof that supported a small bell tower. Though the Bahamian children were poor, they wore shoes and freshly pressed white tops and red shorts or skirts. Their teacher had acquired her education in the strict English tradition, and although she was Bahamian, was intolerant of her people's backward, and seemingly lazy ways.

Jubal did not like school. He listened and was attentive, but the messages that came from the teacher were disconnected and confusing. A single word had many different meanings and implications, and he had difficulty in knowing which was correct. By day's end his confusion had churned into anxiety, and he would run to the sea and throw himself into her waiting arms and swim as hard as he could, as if in the effort, the sea could wash away the contamination that had entered his mind and body. Afterward, he would float and wait for the voice of the sea to waft up and erase his pain. As the school year progressed, and the more his mind pondered words and numbers, the more difficult it became to receive the messages from the sea. Jubal believed that somehow the school was stealing his only true possession, the voice of the sea. The single thing that had given him his sense of union, as well as his identity, with all that was alive (which was everything in the ocean). He began to passively resist the daily lessons that filled his mind with facts which floated unconnected, and information that never amounted to knowledge.

Despite his difficulties, Jubal attended school every day in the promise that the new knowledge his father spoke of would begin to make sense in this new world.

Jubal never volunteered to answer such questions as, " What is a shoe?" For the answer, "A piece of leather that covers and protects the feet," was never at his command. However, there one day came the question for which he unhesitatingly knew the answer.

"What is the sea?" asked the teacher. Jubal immediately raised his hand, and the teacher, curious at his response, for this was his first without prodding, called on him. He stood up and confidently addressed the classroom, "De sea es de life. It breathe an come into da body an play de music. It de play wha all tings come together. It de beauty dat..."

"Excuse me, Jubal," interrupted the teacher, "but that is not the correct answer. Can anyone help Jubal with the correct answer?"

A pretty Bahamian girl in pigtails stood, "De sea is a body of wadda," she answered.

"That's correct Eunice, thank you," said the teacher who turned back to Jubal who was still standing. "Do you understand Jubal that the sea is not all those things. It is a body of water."

Jubal had not seated himself. He slowly shook his head no and said, "De sea es mo den all de words you `av."

The teacher came forward and grabbed him by the arm, "Don't be cheeky with me Jubal Freemountain, you ain't that smart!" She led him to the corner and had him face the wall to the giggles and open laughter of the children. Jubal stayed at the wall for the entire day, suffering his humiliation long after the affair had ended.

Thereafter, he never again raised his hand to answer a question.

Jubal began to spend the better part of his classroom days imagining he was under the water. This he did while holding his breath, occasionally glancing at the clock above the teacher's head to measure his breath-hold. By mid-year he had worked the time up to five minutes and fifteen seconds. Breath-holding became the only activity that gave him cause to attend school; for it was, to his knowledge, the only building on the island with a clock.

Though everyday after school he swam in the sea to cleanse himself and listen for the voice of the sea, the voice grew faint. Even when he swam out to the deep water and dove to the bottom, the voice could scarcely raise itself enough to be understood. When Jubal became certain that education had all but destroyed the voice, he ran away with the intention of leaving the island of Great Abaco altogether.

They caught him in Hope Town trying to hire himself as a bait-boy on a sportfishing boat.

"Wa you run, boy?" asked Ruby Freemountain.

"Da sea where I belong," replied Jubal.

"Da sea no play fo a boy. Scoo da play fo a boy. We got fibe childen, nobody finis scoo. Dis time somebody finis. It gon ta be you, Jubal. Fo you ta know I min bidness, you Fadda gona beat some sents into you."

Wallace Freemountain was not in agreement with his wife, but when it came to contesting her will, he knew where his tongue belonged. He undid the old belt that had been fashioned from the harness of a horse and whipped his son until welts began to drool blood. Jubal never cried, or called out. When his father was through and returned the belt to his britches, he took the boy to the sea and washed his wounds.

Jubal returned to school and every day thereafter swam in the sea to wash himself from the deeper wounds of his education. With each succeeding month the voice of the sea grew fainter. At the end of his first full year in school, the voice had been reduced to a whisper. By the end of the second year, it had vanished altogether.

The reflective, moving light of the sea that had always been cast in Jubal's eyes was extinguished. Wallace and Ruby were concerned that their boy had taken a sickness; for the vibrant energy and joyous spontaneity that marked his spirit, had vanished. The health clinic pronounced him fit, but they had no instruments that could measure the depth of a wounded spirit, much less the loss of a universal voice. To his teacher's delight, Jubal Freemountain listlessly incorporated himself into the daily regime of the classroom and became indistinguishable from the other students.

Jubal stayed in school until he was fifteen years old. In that time he had grown to over six feet, and had acquired a body that was broad in the shoulder and deep in the chest. And while he assumed the handsome Bahamian features of his father's face, he most certainly inherited a body from his mother's side of the family. One day, upon recognizing his size and thus his manhood, he simply walked with his father to the skiff and went fishing and never again attended school. Nothing was ever said either by Wallace or Ruby in this regard. As it was, things had not gone well for Wallace in the past six years. Having lost three fingers to a shark, he was glad to have his son back with him on the skiff.

Jubal returned to the water as if he had never been away. He began to spearfish and take lobster with the hook. Able to hold his breath for over seven minutes, he would spear three fish in a single dive, and on the next breath-hold bring up five lobster. In the deep water he speared grouper that weighed seventy five kilos. The Freemountains became prosperous again, and Jubal's reputation spread from island to island. He became known as the very best diver in all the Bahamas. Perhaps as some said, the very best diver in the world. No one had ever seen better. No one that is, except Jubal Freemountain himself, who, when he was ten years old had understood the wisdom of the sea. Now the voice of the sea was silent, and his only understanding was that he had lost more than would ever be gained again as an adult. There was an empty place in him where once true knowledge had rested.

The pain of his loss compelled him to daily seek out a quiet patch of sand in forty feet of water where he would settle into a sitting position and listen for the voice of the sea. He could hear the clicks of the ghost shrimp, and the grinding of the lobster mandibles, and the snapping of the fish tails, but now the sound seemed to come from all around, and he could not determine their precise origin. He tried to listen beyond the sound of the sea for the language he had forgotten. He listened but his mind had acquired a soft, buzzing sound. Thoughts of his land-bound existence came to him that meant nothing. They swept through his brain like storm clouds in the summer; unceasing and filled with empty thunder.

Jubal spent more and more time listening for the voice. The pain of his loss grew daily, and the Freemountain boat sat higher in the water as fewer fish and lobster were taken. He dove to deeper water attempting to discover the faintest trace of a whisper. One afternoon, after having spent the better part of the day in contemplation of the voice at the edge of a deep drop-off, where no bottom could be seen, he detected a faint whisper, almost a cry, coming from the depths. His heart leaped in recognition, and he lifted from his sitting position and glided to the edge of the drop-off and entered the blue abyss. Soaring as a wingless bird, he descended to the sound that called to him. His joy was such that he did not feel the pressure on his body, or the pain in his ears. At a hundred and fifty feet the voice beckoned with remembered clarity. At two hundred and fifty feet it became as clear as his own voice, and at four hundred feet, in throes of ecstasy, the voice consumed him.

Fiji, Two Fish A Day

*E*VERYBODY DREAMS. Some dream sensible, attainable dreams; others have outrageous dreams of rich fantasy that only a dreamer could live. There are those whose limited powers permit them to only dream of dreaming. There is but a single law to dreaming; if you believe strongly enough in your dreams, they will manifest in your life. Knowing this, the sage cautions, "Be careful what you dream, for soon you will live it."

I dream a lot. Each one wilder than the last. It's almost as if I were testing the law of dreaming. This is the story of a dream. One of being marooned on a beautiful, tropical island. Unlike most such dreams, there is no woman for me on this island. I am a diver and my woman is the sea. It was a dream come true.

I flew all night from LAX and arrived at Nadi International Airport in Fiji two days later. The lost day wasn't missed enough to worry about where it went. I made no plans for this trip, had no reservations for anything, anywhere. Why should I? I hadn't a clue of my final destination.

I called the only name I had, Rick Cammick of Dive Taveuni. He was home. "Sure," he said, "we'll pick you up at the airport. Grab a ride on Sunflower Airlines to Taveuni. See you when you get here."

In the early afternoon they squeezed me into a flight. I think they wanted me and my baggage, which included a six-foot long, by four inch diameter PVC pipe capped at both ends that held my speargun stocks, out of the terminal. I had arrived in Fiji at the height of a military coup, a time when all Americans were advised to stay out of the country. Maybe it was the baggy, paramilitary pants I was wearing; at any rate, I next found myself on a pre-war, twin-engine plane that had just flown in from "Raiders of the Lost Ark." It was an exhilarating forty-five minute flight that climaxed on a dirt runway in the middle of a coconut grove.

Outside the wind-blown shack called the "Air Office," among the black-skinned Indians, and the darkly, chiseled features of the handsome Fijians, was a tall, attractive, fair-skinned woman who waved. Rick's wife Do, had come to greet me. Together we carted my gear to the back of her pick-up and bounced down a rutted, winding, dirt road that paralleled the coast; which, Do explained, was the main thoroughfare on Taveuni.

"Where are you headed?" she asked.

"I don't really know," I confessed. "As far as it takes to never hear a phone ring, or the blast of a car horn, or the whine of a voice over a T V, or radio. A place that won't cost much money. Somewhere I can live off the sea."

"Well," she said, "you're almost there now. But we do have a phone, and a car with a horn, and it will cost you something to live with us. But we can put you up for a few days until you get sorted out. There are plenty of fish, and a great many islands for you to get lost on, it's just a matter of finding the right one, I should think."

I don't intend to get lost," I said, looking out onto crystal water, the bottom of which I could see from the road. "It's the cities that lose me."

She nodded. She knew about cities.

We rode the rest of the way in silence. Shortly, we turned into the beautifully manicured grounds of Dive Taveuni, a resort specifically for divers, laid out atop cliffs overlooking the Somosomo Straits.

I met with Rick that evening after he had returned from his daily excursions into the strait. He said the military coup had created a great deal of upheaval in Fiji, and it might be difficult to find the right situation to suit my needs. Before I could reply, he announced in his thick New Zealand accent, "No worries mate, something will turn up."

And because this was a dream trip, quite naturally, it did.

The following day my wanderings led me to the kitchen and into a conversation with the Fijian cook, Ruthie. In the course of our talk, I learned she too spearfished and, delighted to have a partner knowledgeable of the waters, I invited her to join me that afternoon. She said she would if she could get away from her chores.

Later in the day I found her in the kitchen working over a pile of onions, and without comment she shook her head no, and that was that.

In the evening Do approached and informed me that Ruthie, apparently moved by my invitation had decided to take the next week off and would take me to her home on the island of Qamea. Do added unnecessarily, "This might be just what your're looking for."

The following afternoon Ruthie and I loaded a derelict of a ten foot skiff, powered, and I use the term loosely, by a six-horse outboard. We cast off and began to plow our way south into a twelve-knot wind and a two-foot chop blowing off six-foot swells. We could barely make headway, and in no time were soaked to the bone. Ruthie steered in the stern and I bailed until, near night-fall, we had crossed the Tasman strait and were in the lee of Qamea island.

We ran east for several miles, then swung into a bay shrouded in mangroves. Ruthie poled over a barrier reef and into the thick mangroves. A path had been hacked out of the mangrove, and we snaked our way deep into the muddy channel. The sky glowed a deep crimson in the last light. The heady rot of the mangrove, and sudden screech of an exotic bird burst my swollen senses. All was magic; the stuff of dreams.

The smell of smoke came sharp at a bend in the pathway. Fifty feet ahead materialized a ramshackle dwelling of wood and thatch, with a twisted, corrugated tin roof, that I later learned had been ripped off in the last hurricane. A large, dark-skinned woman of undetermined age smiled in the doorway as we came to a halt at the foot of the raised earthen foundation. Chickens, ducks and a cat trailing kittens wandered out of the doorway; a pig in a wooden pen raised over the mangrove waters squealed in greeting.

Ruthie introduced me to her mother Mariah who, in halting English, warmly welcomed me. Inside, Ruthie's younger sister, Alice, and her sister-in-law Lavenia, the wife of Harvey, were also introduced. Neither spoke English but they nodded and smiled in greeting. The open kitchen was dimly lit by a kerosene lantern and the two girls made lemon grass tea over an open fire and offered dried taro chips while we waited for Harvey to return from a day of fishing.

Mariah had long, wavy hair, indicating European blood, which apparently had not been passed to her children. They, like most Fijian women, had round faces, smooth, chocolate skin, wooly hair and stout, strong bodies.

I sat on a bench fixed to a rough hewn table set in the corner of the kitchen facing the open fire which burned under a sheet of iron set on benches where the girls cut and prepared the food. To my left were two shelves of neatly stacked pots, pans, dishes, cups and silverware. To my right on the opposite wall, were jars of fruits and vegetables in various stages of preservation. There was no electricity, thus no refrigeration or other such conveniences. The Tasman strait was a time warp and the boat ride had transported me back into another century, one which felt strangely familiar. There was tranquility here, a balance that was so obvious it shouted its symmetry in the soft sounds of night overcoming the day.

Behind me, through a door veiled with beads, was the sleeping quarters. Woven palm mats of extraordinary craftsmanship covered the floor. A single bed rested in the far corner with cardboard suitcases stuffed beneath it. A small dresser with a chipped mirror stood in the opposite corner, and shelves covered the two other walls holding all manner of box and bag.

Mosquitoes buzzed the kitchen. They didn't seem to bother the women, or perhaps the women accepted the bites as they so cheerfully accepted their humble surroundings. Ruthie acknowledged that the only store-bought items they used were rice, flour, sugar, soap, and sometimes bread and tobacco.

Mariah took a pinch of leaf tobacco and rolled it in a thin strip of newspaper and lit the end. She inhaled deeply and then let the smoke curl thickly out of her mouth. She wondered out loud what became of the words on the paper she smoked; did they somehow carry the same value inside her body?

As I pondered the question, Harvey poled his skiff around the last mangrove and into the bank. He was wearing a hole-ridden T-shirt that clung to him like a spider web. Blood-stained shorts covered his upper-legs, and a red and white, floppy knotted cap rode to one side of his head. Harvey looked to be in his late twenties, though he could have been older. He was tall for a Fijian, and lean, possessing obvious strength in his arms and hands. He smiled broadly and I liked him immediately.

"Hello, hello, it is always good to have visitors, welcome," he said in crisp Indian tainted English, and clasped my hand warmly, pumping it once. "Just in time for supper, eh. That's good, I have a fish."

The five pound jack was promptly taken and the meal was soon laid hot on the table. The fish was cooked in coconut milk and covered with toasted seeds. There were spinach-like greens called belle, and fried taro chips. The dinner conversation swung from Fijian to English and back in polite small talk. After dinner Harvey got around to asking my intentions on Qamea.

"I don't have much of a plan. When I find a place where I can live cheaply and do some spearfishing to keep me in food, I'll be happy enough," I said.

Harvey smiled broadly and nodded as a child does when holding a secret he can barely contain.

"Right, we see about that. You have your spearguns, eh"

"They're still in the case, I haven't had a chance to reassemble them."

Looking in the direction of Ruthie's boat, he asked, "they are big ones?"

I have two. A small one for reef fish up to 10 or 12 kilos, and a big one rigged with line and a float for the big fish."

Harvey was smiling again.

"Right, I know the place for the big one. Tomorrow, eh?"

"Tomorrow is soon enough for me."

That night I slept under a mosquito netting in a corner on the matted floor. All corners of the floor were occupied, only Mariah slept in the bed. At three in the morning a rooster crowed and on the hour thereafter one crowed until six, at which time they continued non-stop until the sun was well up.

By six-thirty we had finished a breakfast of papaya, homemade bread, and taro porridge. By seven I had reassembled the spearguns, and by eight we were underway. Ruthie brought her dive gear and the three of us, in Harvey's twelve-foot skiff powered by a twelve-horse outboard headed straight out to sea.

Four miles offshore, in blue water, Harvey slowed the boat, looked over and said, "This is the reef." His use of land bearings to find such a small area in the middle of nowhere was impressive. The reef was no more than two hundred yards in length and a hundred yards wide. A needle in a very large haystack.

"Big fish on this reef," said Harvey, "tuna, jacks, barracuda, and wailu."

"What's a wailu?" I asked.

"Spanish mackerel. Very strong. Twenty, thirty kilos, sometimes bigger, sometimes fifty kilos."

"That's a hell of a Spanish mackerel. I didn't know they got that big."

"You're in Fiji now," smiled Harvey, "very big fish here."

I entered the water and the visibility was a hundred and fifty feet, maybe more. It's difficult to accurately judge distance when water is that clear. It was breathtaking. Enormous table top coral heads protruded from a flattened prairie of dead and broken coral at the top of the reef eighty feet down. A school of single stripped barracuda moved lethargically across the reef fifty feet away. Hundreds of reef fish darted about the live coral in tiny splashes of florescent colors like living, crystal prisms.

I no sooner had the gun cocked when out from the head of the reef, coming in from deep water was a very large, silver fish. Although its size belied its species, it looked very much like a mackerel. A wailu, no doubt.

Like any large ocean predator, it was fearless, and swam toward me as it would any intruder. I dropped down to its depth at thirty feet and leveled off. Unhesitatingly, the fish swam into range of the speargun, I aimed and pulled off a good, clean shot. The shaft zipped out, arched, then fell away, dropping beneath the fish which lazily swam off.

The clarity of the water was such that I had misjudged the distance by fifteen feet! My spearfishing brethren back in the States had cautioned me about these crystal clear South Pacific waters, saying perspective is thrown way off. I pulled the shaft in and reloaded; all the while talking to myself. Okay, Carlos, be patient, wait on the fish, be absolutely sure this time.

Swimming over to where I had first seen the fish, I made a dive to attract attention. Out of the infinite blue, three wailu drifted in to investigate. All were large. At a depth of forty feet I waited. The lead fish came in boldly; 10 feet, 5 feet, I could count the scales! The shaft released straight and true and then dropped, nudging the fish mid-body. The wailu didn't even flinch. The point had broken the skin and fallen out, and the fish never broke its drift speed!

Okay, okay, this is a new ball game altogether. New ball game, new ball park, new rules. I've got to get close enough to be able to reach out and touch the fish. Maybe I'm fooled by the size of the fish. Maybe the clear water makes them seem closer than they really are. Maybe the fish is bigger than thirty kilos. It looks bigger.

I'm reloading trying to figure it all out, looking for explanations of the unexplained.

Recocked and down again in the same place, the same three fish drifted in from the deep water. Waiting. Waiting. So close. Wait. Its eye followed me; saw the teeth, big ones, like Caribbean barracuda. Surely the fish will spook; so close. Closer. The gun tracked, like on rails. The point seemed three feet away. I pulled the trigger.

The shaft penetrated high, close to the gill plate. The wailu whipped around and powered for the depths. Not in the lightning speed of a tuna or even an amberjack, but with the freight train power of the grouper, except the wailu was an open water fish. Holding the line I kicked hard for the surface, hoping to turn the fish, or at least slow it. In a single second the slack line was spent and the fish yanked me down as if I were nothing. The power of the wailu took what was left of my breath. I let go of the line and shot for the surface sixty feet up. I had the idea that I would get there in time to grab the float and make my fight from there, but before I reached the surface the float zipped by and I watched it diminish into the depths without perceptively slowing the fish. I couldn't believe my eyes. No forty, fifty or sixty pound fish does that.

"This is Fiji," whispered Harvey, in my mind.

He had seen the float disappear and was there to pick me up in the boat.

"Big wailu. Took everything." I said. "Went off in that direction." I pointed to a breaking reef two miles north. We headed toward it at quarter speed. I fully expected to see the float at any moment. Three pair of eyes scanned the undulating water all the way to the breaking reef and we saw nothing.

"Let's go back," I said when we reached the reef. "Trail a line off the stern and tow me along in the water. We can't lose this fish."

There is nothing worse than losing a fish. A mortal sin for a spearfisherman. Sometimes it happens because the fish is too strong. Usually it reflects an error in judgment- a shot too long, poor water position, a hurried shot and thus misplaced. I didn't realize just how big the fish was. I should have double floated the line the first time I saw it.

"We got to find this fish," I declared to Harvey, "if we have to look `till nightfall."

We went back to the reef and there was no sign of the float. I reentered the water, and while holding the line with my left hand and directing him with the right, Harvey pulled me along at a couple of knots. We ran along the edge of the reef to where it dropped off into blue space, keeping to the general course of the fish. After ten minutes of seeing nothing, another reef materialized out of the blue. I directed Harvey to it, and we ran along its outer edge. A quarter of the way down its length I spotted the float suspended thirty feet down. A half dozen white tip sharks were circling a coral head forty feet below the float where the big mackerel had wrapped the line. The spear shaft laid bare along the outer edge of the reef. There was no sign of the wailu. I pumped up and dove to the coral head. The sharks broke away into deep water as I approached. The line was badly frayed and nearly broken where it ran against the coral.

"No fish?" asked Harvey, when I surfaced empty handed.

"No fish. It either broke loose, or hung up on the coral and the sharks got to it. I think it struggled for awhile and broke free. The shot was a bit high and no vital organs had been hit. It could have gotten off. If the sharks had hit it, I think they would have been twitcher than they were. I hope it got away clean."

The following day we returned to the same reef. The big wailu did not show up, and I speared a small one that underwater looked to be ten kilos, but weighed twenty kilos in the boat. Reassessing the size of the big one yesterday, I would have to say it was well over fifty kilos; which would make sense.

I gave the speared fish to Harvey to pay for fuel. Whereby he announced that if I could spear two mackerels a week, it would cover lodgings on a beach not far from his settlement.

"There are reefs right outside the beach that will feed you, and I will bring water and vegetables and fruit when you need it. You need only tea, sugar, rice and bread from the store."

So there it was, a dream first born of clouds, then breaking through clean and clear into the Fiji sun becoming solid as an island, real as a sandy beach. Ironically, I was handed paradise that only the wealthy could afford, by a man who, in the United States, would be considered poverty stricken. Such is the stuff of dreams.

Harvey steered the boat along the far edge of the coral reefs that fingered straight out from the shores of Qamea. There was no sign of life on the island. Only ebony mounds of lava smoothed by the sea to high tide and then green jungle; pristine and shimmering as if varnished. Harvey pointed to a small beach of white sand wedged between a great lava fissure in the island. Drawing near, the sand beach deepened and two thatched huts appeared, one behind the other. From the nearest hut down to the waterline an enormous fallen tree split the beach in two. The tree was so large that, though barren of leaves, it obscured much of the beach and huts from view.

Harvey killed the outboard and tilted it up, then using a well-worn ten foot tree branch, poled us over the shallow reefs and onto the beach. The white sand was bejeweled with shells and broken coral. We walked fifty feet to the first hut, which was open, having no walls to the rear and west, the fallen tree served as the east wall and was the structure's main support. Along this wall were shelves stacked with cooking and eating utensils, and to the right a small cupboard. In the center of the hut rested a two-burner propane stove that sat on a card table, buried to its knees in the sand. Just inside the seawall a small eating table with attached benches of rough-hewn wood faced the Tasman strait. The entire kitchen and eating area covered fifteen square feet, and was shrouded by a roof of plaited palm fronds. Directly behind the kitchen on a raised cement foundation, stood a bamboo-walled, palm-roofed burr, or sleeping hut. A traditional footbath made of a giant clam shell was set in concrete at the base of the steps leading to the burr. Inside the twelve by twelve foot structure was a table, chair, and a single mattress bed. The floor was partially covered with linoleum, loose and curling at the edges. A beautifully woven grass mat graced the floor in front of the bed. One open, glassless window faced the sea, and one opened to the east looking out over jungle. In the back of the burr, a sheer cliff of black lava, strung with hanging vines, ascended sixty feet to the jungle. The jungle surrounding the beach was so dense that the morning sun had yet to penetrate the trees.

Harvey rolled up the bamboo shutters of the seaward window, and standing there, looking through the open kitchen, past the beach to water so clear the purple corals glimmered like polished gems beneath the surface, I thought that whatever ideas of paradise I had were woefully inadequate compared to the real thing.

Harvey read my mind. "The beauty is everywhere in Fiji, but this place is the most beautiful on the island. We call it Orchid Beach. There are orchids all over the fallen tree, yellow ones. When the leaves grow back they'll protect the orchids from the sun, and that's when they'll bloom. This tree and these orchids have been here for as long as anyone remembers."

Harvey found a broom and began to sweep the floor. I arranged the sheets that Mariah had given me and affixed the mosquito netting. When the place was in order, Harvey stepped back in approval. "Your new home, eh."

From the boat we unloaded the dive gear, a backpack, twelve gallons of water, several papaya, a half bag of rice, some belle, and a old box of tea.

"This will have to last a few days, until I cross over to Taveuni with a load of fish," said Harvey. "You'd better make me a list of what you need aside from the fresh vegetables and fruit." I made a list which included peanut butter, bread, rice, flour, tea, salt, onions, sugar, garlic, lemons, and eggs. Along with the list, I gave Harvey enough money to cover the fuel.

Then without preamble he jumped into his boat and was off. The sound of the motor faded until all that was left were the sounds of birds, and the gentle lapping of the sea on sand. I sat where I had been standing in the sand, perhaps in a mild state of shock in the realization of my isolation from the outside world. Everything I knew seemed so far away that it ceased to exist as reality. I had no past, no history. There was no expectation of future events. I was firmly entrenched in the present, and my mind became incapable of specu- lation. It was as if I had suddenly awakened from a long dream,

I idly played with shells that lined the high tide mark on the white sand beach that was peppered red like the blood of insects. The seawater looked drinkable. From jade-hued shallows the pan- orama swept to lapis-colored water that edged the outside reefs all the way to Taveuni, which appeared as a volcanic emerald rising high into clouds drifting against a cornflower sky. The vastness swallowed me. A sacredness emanated from the pure air and water, and the jungle brought the smell of decay and the indomitable air of the untamed.

I breathed it in, which is really all one can do; simply breathe it in, and let the mind go still.

The following day, in an 1/8 inch full wet suit, (more to protect from the coral than to stay warm in the near eighty-degree water), mask, fins, snorkel, and camera in hand, I entered the water. Skimming along in the shallows, I passed small coral heads blooming like roses in a stone garden, and found passage beyond the coral that lead to deeper water. Here, the water, as clear as liquid glass, was transparent to one hundred and twenty feet. I swam parallel to a forty-foot wide coral reef that extended nearly a hundred feet out into blue water, and floated above the edge, which seemed to shake with life. Fish of every shape and color probed the reef like butterflies on a bottlebrush tree. The coral formations were themselves other worldly; as if Poseiden himself had toppled from a great height and shattered to pieces beneath the sea.

The heaps of shimmering, broken white bones lie in contrast to the browns of the reef, the grays of the dead coral, and the touches of blues and purples of the flowering coral; the rest, the reds, yellows, oranges, and greens were lost in the filtered depths. The vast beauty of this oceanic utopia was grander than my meager senses could comprehend.

The water, as clear as the air, held vibrating fish of brilliant colors that seemed nothing less than the color itself, come alive off a madman's palette. A fluorescent green floated atop a striking purple that crashed into marigold yellow; a dapple of hyacinth sprinkled over a lavender tail, a brush stroke of fuchsia across a wisteria eye, apricot bellies dotted with vermilion. Fish so surreally painted that Salvadore Dali might weep with joy.

I dove down to a pair of orange clown fish, whose vertical white stripes were outlined in black. They danced among the tentacles to whose toxin they alone were immune. "Come and play they invite, the anemone is fine." At eye level with the top of the reef, the fish fluttered by inches from my mask; some with huge heads and scarcely a tail, others with tiny heads and all tail. There were fish that looked like stones, (and stones that looked like fish). The eyes of some fish dominated their heads, while other eyes were lost in the dots of neon scales. There were fish with oversized mouths, and fish with hardly any mouths at all, a fish so thin it looked like a shadowless thread, and one so fat it floated like a hot-air balloon. Some fish fluttered along while others seemed to pirouette about on their tails or heads among the alabaster bushes of coral

I felt like Alice in Wonderland. And like Alice's wonderland, there lurked beneath the spectacle a sinister element. Hidden within this rainbowed universe were creatures that could kill a man in the most unobtrusive way. The stonefish which appears as its name suggests, can fell a man like a tree. The delicious flesh of half the fish could turn the connoisseur to a cold corpse in the morning. Fire corals and fin tips inflict torturous pain when merely brushed. Which was harmless and which was deadly? Like Alice, I wandered in the wonderland with spellbound cautiousness.

Swimming along the reef to its end, I turned east, upcurrent, heading for the far point. Finger reefs extending from the island were separated by a hundred feet of open sand, and each was as the one before it. So it went until I reached the point a hundred and twenty yards east, where three coral fingers extended into a deeper sea. Turning the corner of the last reef, my appearance scattered the large fish that were grazing in the depths; snapper, coral trout, and grouper up to eighty pounds disappeared into the reef. Cruising jacks and small mackerel faded into the open sea, and a school of emperor wrasse dissolved into the sand bottom at a hundred and seventy feet. The sudden activity aroused the interest of several white tip reef sharks that appeared where the wrasse had dissolved. They moved off in that effortless grace seemingly given to all scavengers of both sky and sea. This far reef was a transition zone. Here the strong current brought the glut from the depths which fed the bait, which in turn nourished the large predators. I explored the area which was substantial, and shot a roll of film. It was late afternoon, and I'd yet to shop for dinner. Returning to the beach, I exchanged the camera for a speargun.

With such an abundance of fish, securing a meal appeared to be a simple matter. However, I refused to spear a brightly colored fish which eliminated eighty percent of the population. Nor would I take fish that was not in fair abundance. Without refrigeration, all fish must either be smoked or eaten in one sitting, so size had to be taken into account. I should take a fish weighing more than five pounds. I stalked the far eastern point with the small speargun for two hours before finally settling on an emperor wrasse.

With a weak but semi-accurate pitching arm, I fell three coconuts with beach stones. Then, building a three-walled stone barbecue high enough so the thin green branches used for a grill, wouldn't burn, I laid the meat over the smoking coconut husks as Harvey suggested. The husks were excellent for smoking fish because they didn't flame, and burned slowly for a good long time. After an hour I cut the thin edges around the fillets and ate those while the rest smoked for several more hours. Besides the fish, my dinner included coconut milk, coconut meat, and a bowl of rice. In the months to come this became my basic diet, plus whatever fruits and vegetables Harvey would supply from his garden.

Not long after I had settled into Orchid Beach, I discovered why the fish, in such seemingly virgin waters, appeared so spooky. Several times a week, skiffs, loaded to the gunwales with men, women, and teenagers, came around the island from the west. Sometimes they disappeared around the far east point, and sometimes they stopped off on the point itself to dive for shells and spearfish. The men spearfished, and the women waded in the shallows looking for clams, shells, anything edible they might gather in their hands. The older women stood barefoot at the edge of the coral heads in waist deep water and fished with a handline, as no doubt their ancestors had done centuries earlier.

The weeks slipped by and turned into months, the fallen tree sprouted new leaves, and I continued to dive several hours every day, taking photographs, and spearfishing. Harvey visited every second day, and his generous hands were never empty. He brought pau pau (papaya) which was delicious and had become my breakfast fare. He also brought generous portions of belle, which tasted like spinach, and taro root which I grated and molded into patties and cooked with onions in oil. It had the taste of potatoes and was quite good. He also brought an assortment of sweet yams, tomatoes, and lemon grass for tea. In the center of paradise I lacked for nothing.

Once a week, usually on Tuesday, Harvey came by in the skiff and we went off to the deep reef where the wailu run and I would spear two or three up to twenty kilos to cover my weekly debt. (The big fifty kilo wailu had not returned since that first day). On the days of Harvey's visits, we sat at the table, the island of Taveuni off in the distance, and drank tea, ate coconut, and told our life stories. His interest in America was insatiable, but he had no desire to actually live there; he knew Fiji was paradise, and desired no more in life than he currently possessed.

The Fijians who came by the beach in their boats kept their distance. They smiled and waved when they passed, but never ventured ashore. One day while out collecting shells, I vigorously waved them in. On this occasion they turned to my shore. The women waded ashore first, wearing dresses brightly flowered in greens, reds, and yellows, with head coverings of the same material.

They dove fully clothed in these same clothes. The men, as were most Fijian males, handsome, strong-bodied and gentle-mannered, wore threadbare T-shirts and short pants, which were also their diving apparel. The lower legs of the men and women were a mass of scar tissue. Many had weeping cuts in various stages of infection as a result of brushes against the live coral. All were curious about this white man living on this isolated beach, and they respectfully investigated my holdings with intense interest. The men found the spearguns, and with my permission tested the pull of the rubbers, and caressed the steel and wood. We were on common ground, we were hunters of fish. Though one man spoke a bit of English, and I spoke no Fijian, we were able to speak of the sea and of fish. They invited me to accompany them on their weekly search for seafood, and I readily accepted.

The men dove without fins, gloves, masks, snorkels, or booties. They carried no spearguns. Their equipment consisted of ill-fitting, plastic goggles held together with twisted cloth which they used to tie around their heads. They hunted with a pointed, rusting rod that was propelled by a length of rubber fastened with a loop around the thumb. The tool was remotely similar to the old style Hawaiian sling of bamboo tubing and a free spear. The spear was aimed much like a pool cue; clasped between the second and third fingers of the hand to which the rubber was affixed. The divers were remarkably accurate and generally speared small, hand sized fish. Anything larger could swim off with the spear. In these waters lived tens of thousands of small fish, and while the Fijians favored a certain brown, rather nondescript fish, they speared just about anything that came within range; hence the spooky nature of the entire fish population.

With mask, fins, and snorkel, I spun around the Fijians like a seal, and easily speared the larger fish using my gun, then quietly gloated in my obvious skills. After lunch (we ate the meat from the boiled shells that the women gathered along the tops of the reefs in shallow water), I decided to try diving in the Fijian way and gave my snorkel to one of the men. Without the snorkel my bottom time was cut in half, and because I continually had to lift my head above the surface to gulp breaths could not sustain any concentration. What ever arrogance I had acquired in the morning evaporated. Then I took off my fins to get a real feel of Fijian diving. For awhile I kept up with the others; my frog kicks got me to forty feet, but the ascent was a struggle, and within forty minutes, I retired to the boat thoroughly exhausted and appropriately humiliated. The fellow I loaned the snorkel and fins to immediately doubled his take of fish.

When in the late afternoon, I was brought back to my beach, I felt badly in taking back the snorkel and fins; the Fijian handed them to me with the awareness of the possibilities. It was like exposing him to the powers of electricity, then taking back the generator. The simple snorkel and fins could change his life and the lives of his village immensely. Yet, the harmony and balance in their way of life would have been altered. For their very lack of technology prevented them from taking more fish than they could use. The hunting of food involved the entire family rather than just one or two divers who could do all the work. All things considered, they were better without the technology. I envied the balance of their lives, and had no desire to disrupt it.

The months rolled by. The daily rain coaxed forth a full growth of leaves on the fallen tree, providing shade for the dangling pods of wild orchids that bloomed in vibrant yellows. I had been living the life of a Fijian diver. My skin was dark, my hands, feet, and legs were covered with cuts and infections. I had blended into the seascape and casually attended to my underwater business. I had become accustomed to the white tip and black tip reef sharks that converged on a speared fish and treated them as acceptable annoyances. I was not yet familiar with all the poisonous fish, so I still asked Harvey if a fish was safe to eat when I was in doubt. My breath-holds and legs were such that I was cutting hundred foot dives. A feat I believed no longer possible in my middle years. I had found my paradise, and for the most part believed that I would stay here for perhaps a year or more. Why not? This had become home. Not everyone would be comfortable in such surroundings, but I was a fish who has found his water. There was a harmony to this life that I had found nowhere else; not even while living aboard my sailboat. I think it was the community of the Fijians themselves. We were all divers, and thus were all of the same family. It was as if I, at long last, had found my tribe.

However, no matter how perfect the paradise, one must take into account the unexpected. One fine sunny morning I awoke to a full body paralysis. My muscles had become ridged, my vision tunneled. I had absolutely no strength to rise, and so was forced to urinate there on the floor beside the bed. Something deadly has entered my body.

Harvey visited me the day before, so it was doubtful he would come again. Even if he did, what could he do? The only way to contact the outside world was a boat ride across the Tasman strait to Taveuni, and fuel would have to be found first. From Taveuni I could be flown out for medical treatment. But in the state I found myself, it might not matter. Alone on my isolated beach, in the center of paradise, I awaited my death. Oddly, my mind was particularly sharp, and I was rather astonished at the calm, almost peaceful acceptance of my fate. (In the months, and now years that followed that day, I often look back with amazement at this absolute accord with my death. I believe it came from the day to day, hour by hour, second by second immediacy of the life I was living. It had cleansed my mind of its civilized impurities; fear, anxiety, and a general lack of trust in the universal order of things. I was unafraid of life and so was unafraid of death.)

The next morning I managed to crawl out of bed and get some water. Later Harvey came, and when he realized my condition, he left immediately to find fuel. The following day I wobbled down to the boat and we made for Taveuni. I had all my belongings, including a beautifuly palm-frond mat woven for me by Harvey's wife, Lavenia. On Taveuni the locals diagnosed my illness as ciguatera; toxic fish poisoning. I had eaten a large snapper which had mistakenly passed Harvey's inspection. I was told that the fish had eaten worms that rise from the sea floor during a particular full moon, and which make the flesh of the fish highly toxic. Later it came to my attention that two other Fijians suffered similar ailments, fortunately neither died which is often the case.

It has been said by men far wiser than I, that we are dreaming this life we call reality; that only the enlightened ones are truly awake. If that is so, and I have no reason to doubt that it is not, then it was only during this dream of Fiji that, in all my life, I was truly awake.

c.e.
fall of '87

Tides, Currents, & Other Moving Experiences

These days I find myself up along the central coast of California, near Morro Bay. South, behind the dunes that separate the bay from the ocean, the back bay runs mile upon shallow mile into saltwater marshes and mud flats. Often I'll trek back there to shoot photographs of the great white egret, snowy egret and great blue heron that, among the whimbrels, long-billed curlews, godwits, and willets occupy the vast stretch of half-land, half-water.

Though I have every intention of taking pictures, I usually wind up sitting there in the high grass on the edge of the bay watching the tide come in or go out. One moment there is glistening mud intertwined with small arteries of ribboned, mirrored streams that appear to have fallen from the sky. The next moment there is wind-rippled water vibrating with liquid energy, stretching to far shores. The full cycle of the tides is not something I have ever actually perceived, though I have sat through the entire changes. The subtlety of its movement is just enough to bore me so my mind wanders, and when it returns, the tide has run its course. The magic has been performed, and I never really saw how it was done.

The moon's influence upon the tidal waters of the planet and thus on mankind has always been a source of bewilderment for me. How could something so far away create such powerful and predictable rhythms on the earth's surface? Pliny, the Roman naturalist, theorized the moon's influence on the tides, before 100 A.D. During the 1600's Sir Isaac Newton discovered the law of gravitation and confirmed Pliny's theories, thus scientifically certifying what the oceanic primal tribes had probably long understood. The concept makes sense, I suppose, but the reality still boggles my mind. But then the mysteries of the natural world have always overwhelmed me.

All bodies of water, large or small, are subject to the tide producing forces of the sun and moon. Even inland bodies of water have a regular tide. Most are so small they are usually masked by the wind and weather. Lake superior, for example, has a tide that rises and falls about two inches.

Tides are created by the gravitational force of the moon and sun. The moon's gravity pulls the water nearest to it slightly away from the solid part of the earth. At the same time, the moon pulls the solid earth slightly away from the water on the opposite side of the earth. In this way the moon's gravity produces two bulges on the ocean. These bulges are the positions of high tide. Add to this the earth spinning on its axis, and we usually have two high tides at a given place each day. Near shorelines they may rise six to eight feet. In long, narrow bays and gulfs the tide can rise twenty to thirty feet. In the Bay of Fundy, between New Brunswick and Nova Scotia, the tide rises fifty feet on a good day.

It's all a miracle to me. Consider.

The ebb and flow of the tides generally dictate the daily course of living to the majority of humans (never mind the ocean inhabitants themselves) who live and sustain themselves on nearly every coastline on the planet. We builders of great harbors and miles of breakwater that subdue natural forces, see little evidence of that, but scarcely two hundred years ago it held true for every man jack of us.

These days city folk have lost their connection to the tidal rhythms that have played a significant role in mankind's movements toward new horizons, both externally and internally. Its influence continues to exist nonetheless, and we, in perhaps more subtle ways than can be imagined, are forever moved by them.

Would mankind have ever come into being had there been no moon at all? Would the tides that wash and cleanse the seashore, as blood cleanses the body of its impurities, be stilled. Would then the seas and oceans be lifeless? And if so, this planet could never have blossomed into its rich and varied existence. (Though we seem to be doing our best to wipe her out with our disease of consumption, and its off-spring, pollution, thus squelching the moon's enormous influence on her health and well-being).

What if, on the other hand, the earth had two or three moons as some planets do? Would then the rhythms of the planet be too frenetic? Would man, endeavoring to maintain the pace, burn out and exhaust himself. Would we all be dead of old age at twenty-two? It boggles the mind to imagine a multi-moon effect on cats, dogs, insects, coyotes, grunion, menstrual cycles, lovers, etc, etc. We'd all be lunatics.

One moon is plenty; two tides a day are ideal. It's all perfect. This perfection, I might add, contains all that is beneficial, and all that is destructive, and all that lies between.

I have spent extended periods of my life in the wash of tides. I've lived within their rhythm until I needed no watch to know the time. The tide was either rising or falling. During those years my own rhythm and the earth's rhythm were in sync, and I saw with great clarity my own reflection in the ebb and flow of its crystalline waters.

Once I had mindlessly disregarded the subtle force of a tide with near disastrous consequences. Off the eastern shore of Baja California on the Sea of Cortez, there is a place renowned for its mighty tides. San Felipe was built just about as far north on the Sea of Cortez as was practical, with four-foot-high curbs along the dirt-road main street attesting to the severity of the tides that ran right through the streets on a good day. (As I remember it back in the late sixties and early seventies. Now, I understand there is pavement and condos and an airport and probably fast-food chicken and burger drive-thru's.) Mariners could sail their boats into the boat yard at high tide and work on them during the low tides; no cradles, no booms or winches, simple and direct. The tides ran the town. They were the most dramatic tides in the western hemisphere. In the days before I arrived, tales of children and dogs, chickens and houses being swept out into the Gulf by the out-going tide were not uncommon.

In the spring of '72 it was toward San Felipe that Frank Taylor, Bill Brown and myself returned by boat from a week of diving on Guardian Angel Island, ninety miles south. We got caught in a brutal Gulf storm all the way up and were hit with rain, wind and high seas.

We wore wet suits to keep warm and face masks in the open boat to keep the sea that washed over the bow and windshield from salting our eyes. We had been taking a good pounding for over twelve hours, and were dead on our feet. The only thing that kept me going were thoughts of a hot shower and a good nights sleep on something other than a rock strewn beach.

We pulled into San Felipe's wide bay an hour before dusk. Frank, ever cautious of dragging anchor in roiling seas that pushed directly toward land, dropped the hook uncommonly far offshore. We sat in the driving rain, unable to go below out of the rain for fear of instant sea sickness inside the violently pitching boat. We sat hunched under darkening sky and squall, silent and miserable. After forty-five minutes I abruptly stood and announced I was abandoning ship. Frank, a graduate of Annapolis, who at one time commanded a destroyer in Viet nam, eyed me with glaring disapproval. Under different circumstances I might have shrunk back into my seat; however, the call of a hot shower and dry bedding was more than a match for his withering gaze. So without giving it another thought I packed a bag of clothes in a small satchel, and with fins and in a wet suit, hopped overboard holding the satchel over my head. In the grandest Hemingway style I waved cavalierly to my companions and struck for shore.

The shoreline appeared vague and undefined through the gray curtain of rain that fell in the sunless dusk. I could only guess how far I would have to swim, a half mile, maybe more? Yet with fins and a wet suit I felt indestructible and quickly put distance between me and the boat. My plan was to swim on my back holding the satchel above my head. However, in that position the three foot wind chop broke sea water in my face and prevented me from getting breaths and I had to turn on my side so that I could take regular breaths without swallowing equal parts of sea water.

Within thirty minutes night descended like a phantom, cloaking the sea and air in profound blackness. I stopped to get bearings from the lights on the shoreline. There weren't any. Lights were off to my left. I was disoriented. Apparently I had turned and was paralleling the shoreline. No matter. Righting myself, I located a strong light that appeared offshore, almost directly in line with my position. I assumed it was the boat yard north of the town. I could swim toward shore while watching the light and thus monitor my progress and maintain bearings.

The rain continued to fall and my world became that single light. Though I swam for another half hour, it didn't appear I was making much progress past the light. I stopped and assessed the shoreline. Lights winked from the town at about the same distance the last time I had looked. The realization hit me like John Henry's hammer; the San Felipe tide was going out. I was swimming against it.

I looked back out to sea but in the torrential night there was no sign of the boat, no sign of anything. I headed for the beach, still holding the satchel over my head. I swam for about forty minutes and by the boat yard light was making very little progress. The week of diving and the day-long standing and pounding of my legs had taken a toll. I was not nearly as indestructible as I believed. I was in fact quite vulnerable. It occurred to me that this was the way people died; death by stupidity. When explaining to my family why I had drowned, they would have to say, "he was anxious to take a shower."

I continued to swim, making what seemed to be infinitesimal progress towards shore. The fatigue was becoming overwhelming and out of desperation I began to feel for bottom every couple of minutes. Just to be able to flick it with my fin would have been enough. I knew it was shallow. I would probably drown in eight feet of water. I kept swimming, and to this day I don't know why I kept holding on to the satchel. Maybe because my wallet was inside, (or some other equally dim-witted reason). I decided that in my next touch-try if I didn't feel bottom, I would abandon the satchel and make one, last-ditch, full-out effort for shore.

I sunk as far as my buoyancy permitted, and my fin nicked the bottom. It was still too deep to stand, but it provided hope, if nothing else, and with renewed faith I carried on. A half hour later I was able to stand and walked the last hundred yards into shore. Near the small-boat launching ramp two men got out of their car in the driving rain and squinted at me as I came trudging out of the surf. I registered at the motel still in my wet suit; fins spilling water over the floor when I laid them down to sign in. I showered until the water turned cold, then went down to the bar to celebrate my triumph over the San Felipe tide. After a couple of drinks there came a pounding on the big bay windows that looked out into the Gulf. It was still raining hard and two men in wet suits pressed their faces against the glass. Frank and Bill slogged into the bar moments later. Bill had a half-crazed look and grabbed a bottle of tequila that was sitting on the bar and took a long pull. He slammed it back down and said, "It was all we could do to keep each other going. We gave you up for dead."

If the tide cleanses the inter-waters with its rolling surges, then the currents must be purifying the deep ocean with the velocity of their force. Often currents are referred to as "rivers" within the ocean. This comparison is faulty and misleading. The size, and strength of an ocean current would, by comparison, reduce the Mississippi to that of a creek. The deep ocean, as any mariner will verify, is fraught with peril, everything from fog to hurricanes; but no mariner worth his salt ever underestimates the lethal power of an ocean current.

The largest peacetime loss ever incurred by the United States Navy was the result of a current. In 1923 seven of nine vessels moving south from San Francisco followed the leader into the Point Pedernales rocks. (Point Arguello is frequently referred to as the site of the catastrophe, but I have it on the authority of marine archelologist, Jack Hunter, that this is an inaccuracy.) It was the belief of the navigator in the lead destroyer that the convoy was sufficiently clear of the Point to make his turn east into the Santa Barbara channel. His assumption was based on the speed of the vessel combined with the steady push of the California Current, which, without fail, moves in a southerly direction. However, the navigator did not reckon with an inshore counter-current that pushed water northward with such force that it reduced the speed of the vessels substantially, rendering his calculations worthless. The lead ship and six vessels steamed ashore in the fog and grounded into the rocky coastline.

Thousands upon thousands of ships have similarly engaged an ocean current and met with the same results.

It is little wonder that whenever one speaks of ocean currents, it is often in negative terms. Certainly there are positive aspects to currents. Thor Heyderdahl sailed the Kon-Tiki from Peru to Polynesia via currents in 1947. Later he floated the Ra-II from Morocco to Barbados, putting theories of the expansion of ancient civilizations to interesting use.

In the South Pacific I have witnessed primitive peoples put currents to extraordinary use when navigating about their islands. These same currents were a major factor in the settling of new colonies on remote islands up and down the South Pacific. The

North Equatorial current combined with the Japan current could conceivably have taken islanders from as far south as Borneo up to the Aleutians off Alaska; though this possibility is remote for a number reasons, the vehicle is nonetheless available.

I have long held the belief that we ought to be able to tap into these relentlessly powerful ocean currents as a clean and viable method for producing our own energy needs. Hydro-electric stations, while probably as unsightly as oil rigs, though not a threat to the environment because there would be no waste by-products, could provide such needs. A simple, clean, energy source waiting to be tapped.

Similar to mariners, divers can encounter currents that result in disastrous consequences. Any diver who has put enough time in the water will have eventually encountered a current that but for planning and luck could have ended badly. Such an incident occurred for me one overcast morning at Catalina Island. I had been regularly taking my skiff, the Low Now, up to the west end of the island to this little spot just inside land's end where I had been picking up whites and yellows. There was not another ship on the sea on this gray morning when I dropped into the water just inside the lee to work a string of kelp that had been showing white sea bass. A current was running and the kelp was laying three-quarter down. Under those conditions whites tend to run deep. I didn't even bother to make a dive. The current was pushing me steadily towards the open water, and I went with the flow, intending to drift out to a wash rock that sits fifty feet on the outside of the island and check for yellowtail. As soon as I cleared the lee of the island, the current accelerated noticeably. The kelp was laying flat on the bottom and there were no small fish about. (In the presence of powerful currents there is an obvious absence of small fish. A solid clue that something is amiss.) The current blew me right over the rock within seconds. I immediately turned and headed back toward the island. Behind me was nothing but open ocean for thousands of miles.

Kicking hard, I made it back to the wash rock. If I were to stop kicking for an instant I would have lost the twenty feet I gained. Under the circumstances it was not difficult to project the outcome of this dilemma. I could not sustain intense kicking for very long and so made a shallow dive to the rock ten feet below. I grabbed on to a stringer of kelp, and suspending straight out as a flag in a gale, was able to momentarily relax my legs. However, my bottom time was cut short due to the energy I had expended kicking, and in thirty seconds I needed a breath. I pulled myself along the rock hand-over-hand towards the island for as far as I could then surfaced. Again kicking frantically to sustain position. After thirty seconds of kicking I dove for another rest. I made three such dives, each one shorter than the last. Having reached the point of diminishing returns, I knew that if I didn't try and swim across the small channel that ran between the rock and the island I wouldn't have enough juice to do it at all. Once across I could scramble ashore and walk back to the Low Now that was seventy five yards east.

I entered the channel and seemed to stop dead against the current. Sheer panic generally kills you when under the water, but in this particular case it seemed to sustain my fading legs. I managed to get within fifteen feet of the island and could see kelp and rocks. The panic rush faded and I began to lose headway. In a act born of desperation I aimed the big speargun over the underwater rocks and kelp of the island, and pulled the trigger. The shaft spit out and dropped over and behind an outcropping of rocks. While still kicking I gently pulled the shaft towards me via the shooting line. My hope was that the spear point, which was detachable, would release and toggle into a rock crevice or kelp; something, anything. Fortunately it caught and held fast, and I pulled myself across the channel and onto the island. The twenty-year-old Cressi head I used for white sea bass, because it had three, wide spread flanges to hold the soft flesh of white sea bass, had been my deliverer. A single flange, as slender as a baby's finger, was all that kept me from an open-ocean voyage with minimum accommodations.

There is another aspect of currents that is absolutely thrilling and something of which only divers can partake. I don't care who you are or what you do, but I would guess that at one time or another everyone has had the fantasy of flight. To lift off and fly above the world may well be the most collectively shared fantasy that humankind possesses. I am uncertain of its origin; Freedom? Power? Superpower? Superman? Superwoman? The spiritual inclination to leave our earthbound bodies and ascend to the heavens or other such places that offer relief from an imperfect world? Probably all of these reasons in addition to those which defy speculation. Perhaps if we were more adept at leaving our physical bodies, the sensation of flight would be a gift regularly enjoyed. But, alas, in our arrested development we grieve in our inadequacies.

Grieve no further: We can fly. We do fly. We are able to soar on the wings of the ocean's great currents.

I should define flight as opposed to drift. Anything less than a four knot current is drift. Anything above a five knot current is flight. True flight must possess the element of clear visibility for the sensation to be complete. Such flights of fancy must also be made free from scuba, or other such technical burdens. The ideal flight gear would be a mask, fins, snorkel; no wet suit, no swim suit, nothing else. The ideal conditions would be in seventy-seven degree water with two hundred feet of visibility, and a ten-knot current.

Such conditions, in such flight gear have been my privilege to experience.

Off the western end of the island of Qamea where it comes closest to the Island of Taveuni in the Fiji archipelago, there is a narrow channel of water called the Tasman strait. There, when the tides are right, the current moves like a living thing of awesome power. I stumbled upon it searching for new reefs that might have held big fish. The current picked up and my boatman insisted that once the current started there could be no diving, and that it consumed too much fuel to fight the current. "Five more minutes," I said. The current continued to rise and, as he predicted, I could no longer fight it. He came along side to pick me up and I tossed in my gun and said, "Five more minutes." I dove down to ten feet and began to soar. The visibility was in excess of a hundred and seventy five feet. The water was as clear as mountain air. I spirited over the snow white coral reefs as if they were plateaued mountain tops. I spread my arms, like wings, and banked and lifted and flew like the great lammergeier that haunts the Himalayan peaks. Lifting for a breath on the surface, I maintained visual contact with the sea floor ninety feet down. The boatman came along side, and I tossed him my trunks and dove again, catching the liquid wind down to mountain tops that slid by at celestial speed. This was the flight of dreams, of imagination made manifest. The exhilaration was incredible. Down and up, moving as the frigate on thermals, wings fixed, effortless in flight. Soaring in the ever-present, I had returned to another self. Like the deathless Phoenix, I glided through doors closed to mortals and emerged liquid and fused with the sea. The currents in their velocity had cleansed my soul, and in that flight I was never more at home.

c. e. spring of '92

Swimmer In A Secret Sea

T hough he had been aboard for three days, Dr. Regis Carter had not gained his sea legs, and so stood unsteadily on the bow of the fifty-year-old schooner that had once shipped copra out of Koror in the Islands of Palau. Now the schooner was carrying bags of concrete to the islands of Palau's ancient enemy, the Yap, on the island of Mogmog, on the Ulithi Atoll in the Federated States of Micronesia. With one hand Dr. Carter's pudgy fingers clung to the forestay, and with his free hand he pushed glasses back up his fleshy nose to get a better view of the island as it rose like a felt-green fedora hat out of sparkling blue waters. Dr. Carter was overweight and his feet continually shifted, seeking a measure of balance on the rolling deck. His round face carried the pinched annoyance of discomfort, and his probing, ice blue eyes were in sharp contrast with the disheveled rest of him. "This island," he declared softly, "is the last stop." He had said that before on other ships in other seas, but this time there was fatigue and finality in his voice.

He had come as far as his reasonability permitted. Actually he had crossed over the line of reason and logic, the bastions by which scientists such as himself smugly decreed their paradigms of life and death upon the mass of mankind. This island had beckoned him beyond his reason, and he could feel resistance in his scientific bones. Though this voyage was of three days, the journey itself was of nearly thirty years. It had begun in the early sixties with his first reading of Dr. John Lilly's book, *The Mind of the Dolphin*. He read every book that Dr. Lilly had written, and had read his favorite, *The Center of the Cyclone*, more times than he could remember. Dr. John Lilly was the first man to apply scientific principles in his explorations of the mind of the dolphin in an attempt to communicate with it. And Regis Carter had contracted his disease from Dr. Lilly. He called it a disease because he was helpless in any way to rid himself of his obsession to communicate with mammals whose cerebral hemispheres were so enticingly large and luxuriantly folded. Additionally, there was that huge supralimbicl area in relation to the dolphin's sensory cortex and motor areas. All indications of a highly evolved mammal that was certainly capable of communication, but more, possessed a method of association that would be totally unfamiliar to humans and their concept of reality.

Such were the mysteries that intrigued Regis Carter and had ultimately driven him to obsession. He received his doctorate in Neuroscience and assisted Dr. Ivan Erickson at the Worcester Foundation for Experimental Biology in Massachusetts in the discovery of the nerve cells in the dolphin cortex to be of intricate axonal and dendritic patterns with substantial branching, indicating the resemblance of complexity to that of human brains.

Before that, he had managed to gain employment with Dr. Lilly's dolphin crew and happened to be with the eminent doctor that day in the hot tub when he declared that he would abandon his research of dolphins because he had to learn more about himself before he could go any further. "It is we who must make the change," said Dr. Lilly, "not the dolphins."

Regis Carter was astounded by Dr. Lilly's confession; as a scientist he knew better than that. He wanted to say, look around John, we are the most evolved species that has ever trod the planet. There are no minds greater than our minds. There are minds that may be different, but not greater. And we are obligated by our greatness to explore the possibilities offered us. It is the job of scientists to define reality, so that mankind can go forward and continue to occupy his place at the top of the evolutionary ladder. But he said nothing. In truth he believed that recently Dr. Lilly had drifted off into unscientific realms, and was no longer capable of the objective analysis that his profession required. That night Regis Carter slipped away from the Lilly compound without a word and, after completing his doctorate, joined the Worcester Foundation.

Despite the breakthroughs that firmly established the complexity of the dolphin mind and its potential capacity, Dr. Carter wearied at the microscope. He believed the scientific community was missing the essential element, the dolphin itself. It was through the dolphin alone that the secrets of communication would reveal themselves. It was, he felt, a matter of examining their capacity for mimic, perhaps on subtler levels than had previously been explored, and then employing the proper decoding formula to effect a significant breakthrough.

Initially, Dr. Carter considered what he called, "the Sea Circus'" those establishments commonly known as Sea World, Marineland, and other such centers of marine entertainment. He believed that perhaps dealing directly with dolphins as those trainers had, that, while not scientific in their approach, some element of science might have been utilized and overlooked by those in the scientific community.

In the short time he spent with the trainers he further witnessed the extraordinary capacities of dolphins and whales. But, as he expected, there was no scientific basis in their approach towards communication through language. The dolphins were dependent on the trainers for their sustenance and thus had become little more than marionettes without strings, feeding the country's unquenchable thirst for entertainment. In this brief association Dr. Carter felt party to the theft of the dolphin's dignity. He was certain that they, like humans, were quite capable of being humiliated and degraded. After all they behaved in a pure and honest fashion that embodied much of the traits that humans, in their better moments, held valuable and by which they even defined themselves. As these thoughts coursed through the neurons of his brain, they collided with the image of Dr. Lilly on that last day in the hot tub. He chided himself that such thoughts were speculative and undisciplined; traits of whimsy engendered to common man, and ones which became the undoing of the scientific mind.

It was at this moment that Dr. Carter was struck with the idea that whatever secrets the dolphin had and might reveal would be found in the field. In the wilds of its environment, where man had not the controlling influence. In the field, strict observation of habits and patterns would be discovered, decoding developed, and direct communication finally achieved.

Dr. Carter was able to secure a meager grant based on his previous dolphin research and embarked for the wastelands of Western Australia. There, in the tepid waters of Monkey Mia, it had long been rumored that wild, bottlenose dolphins would venture into the shallow water and interact with humans in a most peculiar manner. Monkey Mia was a ramshackle village of dust-blown trailers and tin-roofed dwellings that, for some unexplained reason, attracted vacationers from all parts of the world, not so much to see the dolphins, but for their health. It was said that there was magic in the air at Monkey Mia, and that the appearance of wild dolphin was just another example of its peculiar enchantment. It was just the sort of place Dr. Carter was seeking. A place open for discovery, and a place where scientific minds had not invested their valuable time, and so perhaps had missed an opportunity.

Sitting on the sand of the bay of Monkey Mia, Dr. Carter observed nine dolphins turning smoothly in the shallow water, the air whistling out of their blowholes, their dorsal fins shining like silver in the high sun. As if in calling, children ran from their trailers, followed by adults down to the water and waded out knee deep, each offering a dead herring to the dolphins which glided in and around them with gentle trust. The children would, when a dolphin came close, reach down and stroke its slick head. Though, not always would the dolphin allow contact, nor would it take the offered fish. An inconsistency that intrigued Dr. Regis Carter.

Every day for a month he sat on the sand and watched the dolphins come and the humans enter the water to feed and interact with them. He would take copious notes of the proceedings and then at night in the glow of his lantern try and detect patterns of behavior by way of a "story board", using color-coded 5x7 cards to trace every movement of each dolphin and human.

The locals had established a "Dolphin Information Center," which, to Dr. Carter's mind, was nothing more than a publicity booth to encourage more vacationers to this God-forsaken bay. The Information Center had given names to a dozen dolphins and were in the process of interpreting their movements and sounds with those characteristic of humans. A notion that Dr. Carter thought was more in the name of wishful-thinking than the hard data required to draw proper conclusions. (And he told them so, which, quite naturally, did not endear him to the small community.) "Dolphin consciousness" was becoming popular with the common man, and he noted in his journal that their small minded view of dolphins and whales was becoming a source of consternation for all who were serious in acquiring the hard facts.

The first week of his second month in Monkey Mia, Dr. Carter ventured into the water himself. While the dolphins came close, they would not allow him to touch them, even after he had condescended to offer a fish. He wrote in his journal that more and more the spectacle at Monkey Mia smacked of a dolphin show that was based primarily on the easy meal. The dolphins were, in effect, simply being induced to interact with humans. Or, perhaps as Dr. Lilly would describe it, they were training the humans to feed them upon request.

Dr. Carter did not include in his journal the feelings of exaltation he experienced the first time a wild dolphin came near, or the child-like expectations he had when he reached out to touch the creature. Unfortunately it had glided away and out of his reach, and he wondered if the dolphin had "read" him as their physiological make-up permits them to do. "Did it see my state of health with its sonar?" he wondered. "Did it sense my emotional imbalance? Did I repel it as a healthy person is repelled by sickness?"

Dr. Carter continued his detailed notes and story-boarding for another month. One afternoon, as an experiment, he swam out to greet the dolphins wearing a face mask, snorkel and fins. As soon as the dolphins saw him they spun around and returned to the depths of the bay. They did not come into shore that day, much to the chagrin of the expectant vacationers.

After that incident hostilities began to unfold. Dr. Carter was labeled an insensitive quack, and he in turn accused the locals of attaching human-type responses to the dolphins by embellishing their movements with childish interpretations such as, "It smiled at me," or, "It tried to speak to me," or, "It held out its flipper and wanted to shake my hand." He laughed in their faces, saying "You would feed a dog and attach major significance to the wagging of its tail."

A week later Dr. Regis Carter was more or less forced to leave Monkey Mia. He wrote in his journal that he was ready to leave anyway for there was nothing in Monkey Mia of scientific value, at least not while human inhabitants were allowed to mingle with, and thus pollute, the dolphin population.

Because he was in the neighborhood, he flew to New Zealand

and sought out the present-day guru of dolphin consciousness, Wade Doak. This was a move he wouldn't have taken a year ago, because Wade Doak was not a scientist. He was a keeper of "incidents", interlock, he called it, of wild dolphins interacting with humans. In Dr. Carter's judgment, Wade Doak could not be taken seriously because he lacked scientific approach. The random encounters with dolphins that he had chronicled were lay interpretations and thus could not withstand scientific scrutiny. Yet he found himself in Whangarei, New Zealand, in a small hilltop quonset hut filled with books and pictures of dolphins, talking with the affable man. Perhaps it was a measure of Dr. Carter's desperation that brought him here, perhaps it was instinct, or maybe just dumb luck. In any case Wade Doak revealed little to Dr. Carter that he didn't already know, save for two rather significant exceptions. One, that the new mecca for studying the behavior of wild dolphins was taking place fifty miles from Grand Bahama on a section known as Little Bahama Bank. And, two, though it was of almost no interest to Dr. Carter at the time, Mr. Doak made mention of a small island in the Micronesia group that still practiced "dolphin calling." The remnants of an obscure myth wherein primitive island people were able, in some manner unknown to European culture, to telepathically communicate with dolphins; which Dr. Carter immediately dismissed as another sort of wishful thinking. However, he was uplifted by the news of human-friendly dolphin that had recently been found in the Bahamas. So much so that he declined a trip offered by Wade Doak out to the Poor Knights Islands to observe dolphin response to music played through underwater speakers, and took the next flight out of Auckland for the States.

Little Bahama Bank lay fifty miles northeast from West End Grand Bahama. It was here that Robert Marx located the Spanish galleon Nuestra Senora de la Maravillas that sunk in 1656. As he and his crew began to salvage the wreck for gold and silver, a school of Atlantic Spotted Dolphin appeared. Over the years the dolphin had come to trust the men, who would take time off from their labors and play with them. Now a generation of dolphin later, they were quite comfortable in the company of humans and are not in need of handouts or any other inducement to become friendly. They were around humans because they chose to be.

In the late afternoon when Dr. Carter arrived on the forty-four-foot ketch, Sea Lion, they were greeted at Sand Ridge by a school of dolphin, which rode the wake of their bow in open invitation. The Sea Lion anchored and the dolphin thumped its hull, encouraging its passengers to join them.

With mask, snorkel, and fins, Dr. Carter slipped into crystal clear Caribbean water that was no deeper than thirty feet. The beauty of the water and the grace of the spotted dolphin momentarily overwhelmed him. Three came barreling up to him, stopping within inches as he winced in anticipation of an impact; then they sprinted away as if shot from a cannon. Taking a breath, he made a dive. Unaccustomed to breath-hold diving he struggled to reach twenty feet where he leveled off and suspended. A single dolphin glided up to within an arm's length away. It looked directly into Dr. Carter's eyes and, as if the connection had the power to suck the very air from his lungs, he sprinted to the surface for a breath. While recapturing his breath the same dolphin swam beneath him, turning on its side so that it might observe him better. Although Dr. Carter at all times endeavored to maintain a scientific point-of-view, he could not repress a strong impulse to reach out and stroke the dolphin. The feeling confused him and muddled his observations. What an odd sensation, he thought. Aside from his mother, who had loved him to a fault, Dr. Carter had never known the sensations of caring associated with love. He had never loved anything but the cold, hard facts of science. So it was with the unease of the unfamiliar that he now observed these wild dolphin at close range.

He dove again, and the dolphin swam parallel to him, slowly turning and letting its tail brush against the skin of Dr. Carter's thigh. Impulsively he reached out and touched its tail-fin. Something akin to an electrical vibration tingled up his arm. As a scientist he knew that such a sensation was an impossibility. Yet he had difficulty convincing himself of that. Indeed, when the dolphin came again he extended his hand, and brushing his fingertips lightly across its slick skin, experienced the same sensation which seemed to charge up his hand and into his arm. The effect so disturbed him that he quickly made his way back to the surface and to the boat.

That night as he lay in his bunk he was a man of two minds. The events of the late afternoon with the dolphin had so distracted him that he was afraid he might not be able to do the objective sort of analysis that was required of his research. Yet another part of him wished to be spirited away by these dolphins. That he had never experienced these sensations before was a mystery, but then Dr. Carter had never known the caring warmth of another creature before, a phenomenon that might have gone a long way in his search for an explanation.

In the ensuing weeks, with his scientific mind fully engaged, Dr. Carter attempted to photo-identify each dolphin on the bank. He had neither the time nor the resources to begin to determine inter-relationships with this group of dolphins as was the standard procedure among researchers, but that was of little consequence, for he was after bigger game.

The dolphin which had first greeted him, and which he named White Scar, because of a long white scar near the dorsal fin, was the most active and certainly the boldest among the group. And it was White Scar to whom he gave his undivided attention. White Scar would often mimic Dr. Carter's moves as he dove and spun about in the water. Though mimic was a form of communication, Dr. Carter was looking for subtle signs that would indicate a deeper level of communication, ones that might provide a breakthrough in bridging the abyss between the formidable brains of man and dolphin.

After a month of intense scrutiny, and coming no closer to an understanding since the day he arrived, Dr. Carter suddenly and unpredictably abandoned his theories of body language. He simply had the sense he was getting nowhere and would never achieve the leap in communication he was searching for. He had never cried in his adult life, but that night he nearly wept with frustration. While lying there in the darkness, his mind empty of his theories for the first time since he could remember, the face of Wade Doak appeared as clear as a full moon in his mind's eye. And the seed that Wade Doak had casually planted began to quickly germinate. Perhaps it was a measure of Dr. Carter's desperation to even acknowledge the possibility of telepathic communication with dolphins. As far as he knew, he had never personally experienced the phenomenon, though he did acknowledge that something as ethereal as telepathy could be experienced, and the experienced would have no knowledge that it was operating. Or that particular gift may have been misplaced on a rung of the evolutionary ladder. Or perhaps, as Dr. Lilly might have suggested, mankind had not yet reached that rung, at least both feet were not yet firmly planted where they should be. In either case, it was clearly time for Dr. Carter to make a radical shift in his hypothesis.

Dr. Carter began to float for hours in the water intently observing White Scar resting on the white sandy bottom as if in sleep; in his mind he formed the words, "Come to me," in vivid white letters against a black background. He was awaiting a sign, anything, even a glance upward would have been enough to give him the courage to move forward with this theory.

He lay in the water for hours, days, and finally weeks. No sign was forthcoming. In the end he was not even sure what he was looking for, or if White Scar had actually laid in the sand or had swum by his side. He was feeling numb and blind.

In the final hours of the last day he lay floating on the surface, still feeling dumb and blind, unmindful of a cross-current that was sweeping him away from the boat. White Scar had appeared and rose beneath him, nosing Dr. Carter's arm out from his side so that the dolphin's dorsal fin had lodged into his arm pit. From his other side came the dolphin he named Lucy, which did the same. Now hooked as he was, the dolphin swam easily against the current towards the boat which was now nearly a mile and a quarter away. Dr. Carter lay limp between the two dolphin, unable to decipher what, or why, they where behaving in such a manner. It wasn't until they encountered an inflatable chase boat, heading directly towards them, that the dolphins let him go. He realized that they were bringing him back to the boat, and quite possibly prevented him from being swept away by the current and perhaps even saved from a horrible death.

The journey to West End Grand Bahama seemed incredibly short for Dr. Carter. He sat in the bow of the Sea Lion attempting to piece together the events of the last seven weeks. Something was there, just out of reach, almost tangible, yet could not be grasped. It floated beyond his comprehension. He felt he was staring right at it, but could not see it. He was left with the single, clear realization that he was finally heading in the right direction. He had found a new path, one he had never taken before, and it was exhilarating.

The green island of Mogmog in the Ulithi Atoll in the Federated States of Micronesia loomed off the bowsprit of the schooner, and Dr. Carter made his way to the wheelhouse. The captain was an old Portuguese, short and dark, with thick gray hair and a three-day growth of beard.

"Soon, I let you go. Drop off my cement and pick up my money."

"What's the cement for?" asked Dr. Carter.

"For a pier. They going to build a pier for a resort for divers. Pretty soon, this place be stinking with foreigners, they won't need me anymore. They'll change this island into Tonga. Ruin it forever."

Dr. Carter nodded in agreement, as if stinking foreigners did not apply to him. Among all the archipelagos of Micronesia only the islands of Yap endeavored to maintain their ancient traditions and values. Here, he was certain that if there were secrets of communication with the dolphin, as Wade Doak had speculated, he might find what for so long he had been seeking.

"Where do I find this friend of yours?" asked Dr. Carter.

"He comes out in the skiff to unload the bags of concrete. Name Jimmay."

The schooner dropped anchor inside the lagoon of the atoll in white sand. Three skiffs rafted to the schooner and brawny, brown skinned men jumped on board and began to unload the ninety pound bags of cement as though they were pillows of down. The captain had brought Dr. Carter's single bag to the gunwales, and pointed to a middle-aged man at the outboard who was shirtless and had a brightly colored length of cloth wrapped around his waist and between his legs. "That's Jimmay," he said, and waved.

Dr. Carter lowered himself into the skiff and the captain tossed down his bag. Jimmay Kugfas (Koofas) had broad shoulders and brown, kinky hair, a wide nose and full lips. His almond shaped eyes gave him the look of an oriental, which was possible thought Dr. Carter; there was Japanese, as well as some German and American blood running through the veins of many Micronesians. His most distinct feature, however, was his teeth. They were stained a deep red, as if he were drinking blood. Dr. Carter had to keep himself from staring at the smiling man who ran his skiff up on the fine, white sand of the beach.

Jimmay sat in the sand while other men, similarly clad, and red toothed, unloaded the boat. He spat red juice into the lagoon that was like glass and as clear as a child's eye.

"You want betel nut?" he asked Dr. Carter, exposing a juicy ball of red on his tongue.

"What is it?"

"Betel nut. Split em' open, put a little crushed coral down the middle for the lime, and wrap em' in pepper leaf. Stick em' in your cheek."

"Uh, no thanks. My interest is in dolphins."

"You want to look for dolphins?" asked Jimmay.

"No, not exactly. It is my understanding that your people can actually call dolphin in from the sea. I'd like to speak to a priest or someone in that regard."

Jimmay shook his head, "It's not what you think. The man who calls would not speak to you about such a thing. You must know the proper questions, eh."

"I'm quite familiar with dolphins. I know precisely the questions to ask," replied Dr. Carter.

Jimmay spit red juice again. "It's not questions of fact, but questions of power."

Jimmay turned and looked full into Dr. Carter's eyes, who blinked uncontrollably.

"Yes, well I expect I'll have to gain his confidence. My interest is in science, and that might encourage him to give me some answers."

Jimmay laughed. He shook his head and laughed at this white man who was wearing an oversized straw hat and sunglasses, trousers and a cotton, long-sleeve shirt, who was asking for something of which he knew nothing and would never know, even if somehow he were to stumble over it. Despite Dr. Carter's obvious shortcomings, Jimmay liked him. He liked everybody.

"You come to my village. I take you in the water, maybe you learn the right question, maybe not."

"All right, Jimmay," said Dr. Carter. "If you think that's the best way."

Jimmay rose and pointed inland as if to follow. "It is the only way."

"I am anxious to start. When do we begin?" asked Dr. Carter.

Jimmay shook his head as if to silently declare that this man was going to be a very poor pupil. "We don't worry about when and where on Yap. We sit back and let the world come. We don't try and push it, eh."

They headed down a well-worn path of hand-laid stone, bordered on either side by high jungle. Shortly they came to a village of smouldering fires in open huts and houses of thatch roofs on raised cement foundations. At the entrance to the village was a large stone the size of a small car with a hole carved out of its center. Dr. Carter pulled out his camera and took a picture.

"It this a totem of some kind?" he asked.

Jimmay sat on his haunches and spit red on green leaves. "That's Stone Money," he said.

"Oh," said Dr. Carter, "someone would have to have a very large purse to carry that around." Then he picked up his bag and prepared to enter the village. Jimmay had not moved, and Dr. Carter who was tired from his sea voyage waited with a degree of impatience.

Jimmay continued to stare at the large rock with the hole in it. "This rock cost sixty men and took nine months to make. It is very valuable to my village. It was made after a battle on Palau and was carried on a raft that came seven hundred miles across the water to here."

"Well that's quite a feat." said Dr. Carter, genuinely impressed. "How long ago was it accomplished?"

Jimmay got up, and walked past Dr. Carter saying, "You asked wrong question."

They passed a dozen thatched houses and came upon a large building that Jimmay said was the men's house. He also said that the women's house was located at the other end of the village. Jimmay stopped to speak to a group of men who were erecting a new house made of stripped logs and milled two by fours, giving Dr. Carter an opportunity to take in his new surroundings. Bare-breasted women wearing wrap-around skirts sat in the shade of high-pitched roofs of plaited palm frond, burnishing the same leaf across a round rock that rested in their lap. The young women were strikingly beautiful and were without a hint of self-consciousness. Clusters of children gathered with polite expectancy and Jimmay had to shoo them away. Everywhere people smiled as they went about their chores. Jimmay led Dr. Carter through the village and into one of the smaller huts that was but a single room covered with palm matting and several woven rugs of intricate patterns in greens, oranges and blues.

"This is the living house," said Jimmay. "You sleep here in this corner. Everyone in the family has a place. We eat at the kitchen next door."

Dr. Carter had not eaten all day and asked what time meals were served.

"When the food is ready," smiled Jimmay.

"How do I know when it's ready?"

Jimmay shrugged his shoulders, "It is something everyone knows, but I don't know how they know. The quiet voice knows everything, eh."

Dr. Carter was puzzled, "Which voice is that?" he asked.

"If it does not speak to you then how can you know it?" answered Jimmay.

Dinner was prepared on a rough-cut table in the eating area and Jimmay had to fetch Dr. Carter in the sleeping hut so that he might have something to eat. There were yams, fried breadfruit, and fish sprinkled with pepper and tomato, which were grown in gardens that surrounded the outskirts of the village. The cooking was done over an open flame by two young women who were the daughters of Jimmay's sister, and who were supervised by his mother Tasa who had tattoos over her arms and back and across her shoulders. Jimmay said that her family had great wealth when she was a young girl and the tattoos were a sign of wealth.

After dinner Jimmay escorted Dr. Carter down to the men's house at the west edge of the village. Its high-pitched ceiling was beamed with sturdy trees stripped of branches and held together with bamboo bindings. Suitcase-sized boulders, half-buried in the earthen floor, formed a circle around a fire pit. The men who sat on the boulders were introduced to Dr. Carter and welcomed him with friendly smiles. "Mugathane," they said in greeting, and offered a warm beer. The men conversed in Yapese and occasionally Jimmay would convey the gist of the conversation, which was little more than village gossip to Dr. Carter; a new house was going up, soon work on the pier would begin, a man caught a great fish outside the reef that morning.

The men were smooth-skinned, muscular, and at ease in their near-naked bodies. They, like Jimmay wore bright bolts of cloth around their loins, the younger men giving a flourish to their garment by leaving a tail that began at the small of their back and floated toward the ground. Dr. Carter was intimidated by their individual and communal strength. There was not a sign of competition among them. Each individual carried respected weight. It was nearly an hour before he realized that the chief of the village had been sitting in on the gathering. Dr. Carter had finally recognized him by the subtle deferring of opinion by the more vocal of the group. Such an occurrence would never have taken place in western culture, noted Dr. Carter. Egos would be competing for status and dominance. There was no such competition here; mutual respect was clearly evident. It was almost as if the men were of one mind.

Dr. Carter asked Jimmay if the chief was the one who called the dolphins. The conversation among the men immediately ceased, the man who was the chief rose from his stone seat and left the room. Jimmay also stood and motioned to Dr. Carter to follow him out.

"That was a mistake, boss. Now Chief Luktun will be cautious with his power while you stay here."

"I didn't know he understood English."

"He doesn't; you showed him your mind, eh. That is what he understands."

The next morning Jimmay escorted Dr. Carter down to the lagoon. Jimmay's dive gear consisted of a pair of goggles, long pants and a long-sleeve shirt, while Dr. Carter wore his mask, fins, snorkel, and a lycra body suit to protect him from coral cuts. The water was warm and clear as glycerine. The visibility was in excess of a hundred feet. Sixty yards from shore there appeared a long coral reef that rose off the sand bottom as a mushroomed cloud housing thousands of butterfly fish of vibrant color, which fluttered delicately above the flowered heads of coral. Jimmay dove, frog-kicking his way down to forty feet and the top of the reef. He moved with easy grace as if he were not dependent on the air in his lungs. Deceived by the clarity of the water, and the nonchalance of Jimmay in the depths, Dr. Carter impulsively made a dive, and by the time he reached the reef was completely out of breath. Immediately turning, he rushed back to the surface. While recapturing his breath, Jimmay continued to prowl along the edge of the reef, as if he had all day. Finally he lifted for the surface and casually frog-kicked his way to where Dr. Carter floated. They swam down the reef and came to another reef that rose to twenty feet from the surface. It was not nearly so lively with fish as the deeper reef, but was accessible to Dr. Carter's limited abilities. Before he dove he asked Jimmay, "What exactly are we looking for?"

"Look for nothing," replied Jimmay, "and see what you find."

Dr. Carter dove to the reef and hung on to the coral with gloved hands. Fish danced in and out of the coral labyrinth in their endless business. The spectacle was nothing Dr. Carter had not seen before, but the excessive visibility gave him the sense of unbridled suspension, and in its minor disorientation he found a certain delight.

The dives he made in the next few hours had somewhat stilled his active mind, yet he continued to wonder what any of this had to do with dolphin calling.

When finally they left the water and sat on the beach in the shade of a beach hut, Dr. Carter asked that very question.

Jimmay did not answer his question, but instead asked, "Did you hear the voice of the ocean?"

"What do you mean by voice? Like the fish sounds in the ocean?" questioned Dr. Carter.

"No, the voice," said Jimmay patiently. "The ocean speaks. It is like a song, but sometimes like a whisper."

"Well, I heard the usual snapping of fish tails and such, but nothing like a song. I didn't know I should have been listening for anything."

"It cannot be heard with the ear, eh. It is felt in the high stomach, just below the chest. That is where the song of the sea is heard. You must hear the song before you can know anything about dolphins."

Such an idea was, at first, summarily rejected by Dr. Carter. The logic of it alone caused him to heave a deep sigh of dismissal. Yet he could not ignore it entirely. He had come too far, and seen too much to reject anything out of hand, no matter how obscure.

"Exactly how is it possible to hear or feel such a sound?" asked Dr. Carter.

Jimmay did not answer right away. He looked out across the lagoon, lifted his head and smelled the wind that came out of the northeast.

"When I was a very young boy my father told me of the song of the ocean. He said that I must let all the life in the sea come into my stomach. When it began to happen I got very scared, the life in the sea is very powerful; it is too much for the body of a boy or man to take in at first. The body, out of fear, throws it off, and will not let it enter. It must come in through the small hole where you were attached to your mother in her stomach. The ocean slips in a little bit at a time; then slowly the hole becomes large and the sea fills your stomach and rises to your chest and presses against the bottom of your heart. That is where the sound is heard. Once that place is open, then you hear the voice and maybe understand the language."

Dr. Carter knew he was at the end of his journey. He had traveled every path conceivable and in the end it had led him here, which was, he considered, perhaps nowhere. Had he heard Jimmay's tale a year ago he would have laughed in his face and walked away. But now, if for no other reason than to find his way back into the good graces of Chief Luktun he was more than willing to go along with a such a notion.

"Okay, let's go for another dive," said Dr. Carter.

"First we eat, eh. Then we go to the east side, near an opening to the outer water. The voice is always louder over there."

In the weeks that followed, Dr. Carter dove the inner reefs of Mogmog, awaiting the voice of the ocean. He would dive on a breath-hold behind Jimmay and hold on to a coral head and suspend, letting his body thoroughly relax and attempt to quiet his mind by blending it into the stillness that surrounded him in the water. He would feel his heart rate slow and a deep sense of well-being would accompany him. There were times in those weeks that he actually forgot that he was under the water. He began to see the inhabitants of the reef in a way he had not seen them before. They were not as remote or other-worldly; though sometimes, when the light was right they appeared as shining particles of pure energy, like stars in deep space. The ocean in the quiet of his breath-hold seemed to be breathing like a great living thing of benign and wondrous beauty.

On their walk back to the village after a dive one morning Jimmay asked Dr. Carter, "You ever do any spearfishing?"

"No, I've never tried it. It's not something one can master in a day, and I've never had the time or inclination to try."

"On these islands every boy learns to spearfish. It's part of how he learns to feel the sea and hear the voice. We take the light and spearfish at night when the fish are slow and blind to the diver. Tomorrow night we go, eh."

The moon had not yet risen and the three skiffs rested on what appeared to be a sea as black as tar. Dr. Carter could hardly see Jimmay who sat at the outboard. The white trim of the other boats were scarcely visible, and men standing in the boats were only apparent by the sound of their voices. Each man was armed with an underwater flashlight and a crude hawaiian-type sling that propelled, by way of surgical tubing, a thin, rusting spear through a hollowed out piece of bamboo. Though he was offered a spear, Dr. Carter refused it, afraid that he might accidently shoot somebody. Now, as the men slipped into the water and their lights were turned on, giving off an eerie incandescent glow that distorted them into ghostly, liquid shapes, he wanted a spear, for he was feeling his vulnerability.

Jimmay went into the water first and Dr. Carter followed close behind. The water seemed warmer than the water of day, and embraced Dr. Carter in a pleasing way, but its utter blackness clutched at his throat, restricting his breathing, and he blew great shivering blasts of inhales and exhales through the snorkel tube. He fumbled for the light switch, and when finally he turned it on, a thin beam of light, like an unsteady finger reached out for perhaps fifteen feet before it was absorbed into the ink of the sea. Through the beam, like an apparition, swam a black tip shark. Dr. Carter froze on top of the water, feeling more vulnerable than before, for now the sharks knew where he was, and could come from any direction at anytime and attack at will. If the light didn't draw them in, then certainly the twitching death throes of a speared and bleeding fish would do so. He looked up for the boat that could not have been more than thirty feet away, but could not find it in the coal-blackness of the night. He had no choice but to stay with Jimmay, and swam closely behind in the stiff, jerky, movements of the frightened and the blind. His body had tightened, and his stomach muscles endeavored to contract and pull him downward into the fetal position. He could barely feel the water that encased him, much less any vibrations that the sea was giving off in the way of a sound or voices. He realized that this confined and rigid state was more or less the one he had always operated in, both in and out of the water. Its source he recognized was fear. Out of the water it was a fear of being ordinary, in the water it was a fear of the unknown.

Jimmay made a dive and his light caught a slow moving fish in its beam. The spear darted out of the blackness and struck the fish, which quivered violently in the light and then an instant later, Jimmay had his hand on it and was coming to the surface. He swam to the boat and Dr. Carter followed, somehow Jimmay knew exactly where the boat was anchored and when he tossed the fish into the boat Dr. Carter climbed in as well and sat silently on the seat. Jimmay stayed in the water and held on to the gunwale, observing him. Dr. Carter knew his fear was obvious and gave off a stench. He couldn't hide from these people, and didn't try.

Despite his set-back from the night dive, Dr. Carter was, by the end of the fourth week, experiencing the underwater world like he had never experienced it before. What was once an alien environment was now almost home. He believed that it was the breath-hold that made the difference. The technology of scuba had been an unseen barrier between him and the living sea. Now it almost felt that the sea were washing through him, cleansing him, giving him new strength. He felt calm in the water and in possession of a new power he could not name.

Despite this sense of bonding with the waters of the lagoon, he did not hear or feel the omnipotent voice of the sea in his chest.

At the beginning of the fifth week, after having surfaced from a dive, he and Jimmay were recapturing their breaths on the surface. "Big manta ray coming, be by here very soon," said Jimmay.

But no manta ray appeared and they dove again. Thirty seconds into the dive a great shadow darkened the area where they suspended just above the reef. A manta ray of several thousand pounds glided overhead, its white belly glowing and its great wings scarcely giving evidence of movement. The sighting was spectacular and leeched the breath from Dr. Carter's lung; and as soon as the manta passed their position, he lifted for the surface, and Jimmay followed.

"How did you know that the manta ray was coming?" asked Dr. Carter as soon as Jimmay surfaced. "You couldn't have possibly seen it, it was minutes away."

"I feel it," replied Jimmay matter-of-factly.

"Where did you feel it?"

"Same place I tell you about, up in the stomach."

"What did it feel like?"

"The manta ray feel like an itch inside the bone. The manta ray very powerful, so the itch is strong."

"Can you feel other creatures?"

"Yes, the turtle, the tiger shark, the dolphin."

"What about the reef sharks here, the white tips and black tips? Can you feel them too?"

"Not the same. But I know where they are in the water, my skin tell me that."

In a sudden burst of absolute clarity, Dr. Carter realized that his pursuit of the ocean voice would ultimately be fruitless. I am a swimmer in a secret sea, he said to himself, and can never know the truths that this man, or these people understand.

"Don't quit yet," said Jimmay, as if Dr. Carter had spoken aloud. "It take many small steps, eh. Everyday is another step."

The following week Jimmay and Dr. Carter ventured further out into the lagoon, nearer the split in the barrier reef that emptied into the open ocean. Jimmay wanted Dr. Carter to get a feel of the force of the sea current, and become familiar with a wilder ocean that was more inclined to force entry into his closed stomach. At the very least Jimmay wanted him to experience some of the more obvious elements of the ocean: the tide change, the cross currents, and the subtle temperature changes, perhaps even the up-swell of a deep reef.

The water was spectacularly clear and it made a reef at forty feet accessible to a dive. Dr. Carter never believed he would be capable of diving to such a depth on a breath-hold. In the deeper water the pressure seemed bent on absorbing him, and he felt less resistance to the ocean than ever before. In fact, the closer he got to an understanding of the sea, the more he realized the impossibility of hearing its voice. It was enough to be down at forty feet and sense the ocean with his skin and eyes.

Jimmay gently grabbed Dr. Carter's shoulder and gave the signal to ascend. On the surface Jimmay said in a calm voice, "a tiger shark has come into the lagoon. We stay close and go back to shore."

Dr. Carter did not panic when he heard Jimmay's prediction. Nor did he doubt its validity. They began to swim slowly back towards the island. Within a minute, a large, bile green shark, wove among the coral heads directly beneath them. Dr. Carter had never been in the water with a shark so large and menacing looking. It was close to twelve feet long, thick and powerful. He felt his body close down in fear, and attempted to talk his way free of the paralysis that was overtaking his body. Jimmay stopped swimming and dove to meet the shark, suspending in the water just in front and above it. The tiger shark turned slightly to its right and eyed Jimmay as if he were a shark or some other creature that had to be reckoned with. Then the tiger continued its turn and headed back to the deep water. Jimmay rose to the surface and led the way back to the island without a word.

When they were sitting on the sand, Dr. Carter asked, "What happened out there, what did you do to make the shark go away?"

Jimmay smiled, "It is something that you know I send it back to the deep water."

Dr. Carter nodded in agreement, "You're right. Two weeks ago it would never have occurred to me. In that time I've not only witnessed your powers and abilities in the water, I've also seen that I'm incapable of understanding those powers, much less acquiring them. I've come to the realization that there's another way of knowing, another kind of intelligence of which I am thoroughly ignorant. I've come to the place that Dr. Lilly had arrived at years before. The exploration shou'd not be into dolphins, but into ourselves. My colleagues will continue to observe dolphins, identifying individuals and plotting relationships. Trainers will continue to force their own precepts down the throats of the dolphins, and none of them will ever get any closer to communication than they already are, which is nowhere. Science, with its rules, axioms, and structure, all the elements that have given me a sense of sure-footing, is as slippery and inconclusive as the dolphin itself."

That night in the men's house around the fire, Dr. Carter spoke to Chief Luktun.

"Chief, I wish to express apologies for my intrusion into your village with my western ideas. Jimmay has demonstrated powers that are beyond my understanding, and he has said that your powers far exceed his own. I've no doubt of that. My mission here was to discover your secrets of the calling of the dolphins. I now see that those secrets are beyond my western mind. Everyday we in the west are moving further away from that understanding. I fear that as our civilization encroaches onto yours, as it will when the Dive Resort is built, that your knowledge of the sea will one day be lost, and never be regained. Chief Luktun nodded, not so much in his acceptance of the man's confession, but in the humble way he presented it.

Billowing cumulus sailed across the azure sky as Dr. Carter loaded his bag into Jimmay's boat. The group of men from the men's house had come down to the beach to see him off. This pleased Dr. Carter, and he solemnly shook their hands and thanked them for their generosity. As he returned to the boat the door of the beach hut swung open, and all eyes turned to the sound.

Chief Luktun glided out of the hut and fell to his knees at the edge of the water. He slowly opened his arms to the horizon and tilted his head towards the sky.

"They come," he said in a hoarse voice, "they come."

Everyone turned to the lagoon and Jimmay pointed. The water churned and boiled as rolling gray shapes bounded in from the slit in the barrier reef. As they neared the shore the dolphin slowed and lolled in the shallows. Jimmay and the men waded out knee deep to greet them and caressed the seemingly mesmerized dolphins from head to tail. As the shoreline filled with the rocking bodies of the dolphin, Dr. Carter sat in the sand with great tears rolling down his cheeks, and sobbed like a child.

The Dream Dive

All fantasy has elements of reality. All wishes are grounded in possibilities. The fabric of reality is stitched with surreal threads, and from those threads our dreams manifest into actuality.

Having said that, I am about to embark on a journey that embraces all the above.

I have long held that if given a single wish, one that knew no bounds of time or space, (if, in fact there are such limitations), I would return to a year before man had sullied the ocean with his flotsam of progress and make a dive. I figure five hundred years ought to be enough to find the west coast, of what is now called the United States, free of the tamperings of man. Though back in 1492 there lived along the specific piece of coastline I have in mind, a group of Native Americans that later became known as the Juaneno, so named by the Spanish after the mission of San Juan Capistrano, which was built in their territory. Actually the Native Americans were Shoshone. I prefer to call them what they called themselves, Shoshone. But they were few and broken up into small groups, and as near as I can tell they didn't work the seashore as diligently as their brothers the Chumash, who resided further north. Though neither group made so much as an infinitesimal mark on the environment in terms of actual impact; so for all intents and purposes the water would be as pure as it had been for the last couple of million years.

On such a journey I would travel light: a wet suit, weight belt and weights, face mask, snorkel, and fins. There was a time when I would have taken a speargun, a very big speargun. For in 1492 I figure the fish would be very big. But these days the spearing of fish holds less interest for me than when I was young, and besides I wouldn't want to interfere with future events by rocking the boat of the past. Might I, in the elimination of a single fish, accidently wipe out a species? Who knows? After all, the fabric of reality is stitched with surreal threads. So I would leave the speargun behind. I might consider taking a camera, but then I would be interfering with my own direct experience of 1492. In the taking of photographs I might miss the entire journey. I mean, why go to all the trouble of breaking through the time\space continuum with a lifetime wish and then fall short of the experience. So no camera either.

Where, might you ask, am I going? A fair question. This could well be your fantasy. At least you can fantasize that its your fantasy. No harm in that. It is unlikely we are going to the same place. So fill in the appropriate location where applicable. Me, I'm going to Laguna Beach on the rocky coast of Southern California. I began to dive there when I was a teenager. I loved the place back then. There were scarcely any people, and almost no divers in the mid-fifties. I honed my free-diving skills in the waters of Laguna Beach. As a kid I wished I could live there so I could dive whenever the water was clear and begging to be explored. Eventually I moved to Laguna and was able to live out my kid's fantasy. I did dive everyday, or almost everyday, whenever the water was good. I came to know every reef from Crystal Cove south to Tenth Street, in South Laguna and further south to Salt Creek, before it was renamed Monarch Bay. (Not renamed by the Spanish missionaries, but by real estate developers, which, I suppose in the twentieth century amounts to the same thing.)

Right off Pacific Coast Highway, just south of what could loosely be called the center of Laguna Beach, was Cress Street. The Cress Street reefs, well known to surfers and divers alike, but not for the same reasons. There were three reefs, each breaking water; twenty yards of water separated the shoreline from the first reef, and forty yards of water separated the first reef from the second, and about fifty yards of water separated the second from the third. The furthest reef drawing a bottom of fifty feet. This last reef extended further out into deeper water by virtue of a thick kelp bed that housed a variety of fish. I had speared yellowtail out there, white sea bass, calico, sheepshead. Closer to shore, just past the first reef schooled corbina and the occasional halibut. South of the reefs, all the way to Woods cove was a long bay that was honeycombed with rock outcroppings and smaller submerged reefs. Lobster, on those little reefs, not many now, they've been worked pretty hard by the trappers, but I've pulled my share out of that bay. When I left Laguna Beach for good in 1981, everything was picked over and it was hard to find a legal lobster anywhere.

I have dived in clearer, richer waters than Laguna Beach. Living off my boat at Catalina Island all those years produced some wonderful experiences. There was the magic of the Gulf during the seventies, and later the South Pacific. All for the most part superior to Laguna Beach. And yet I am drawn to Laguna as a child to its mother's skirts. Perhaps it is home and the other places are not. Or maybe it's because the beach dive has always held a special appeal. There is nothing quite like swimming out from shore and spearing a nice fish or grinding out a sack full of lobster, abalone or scallops, and returning to the shore and the warm fires of a homestead to lay the gifts of the sea upon the dinner table. During those years in Laguna I had time to locate small, undiscovered reefs that were usually loaded with some sort of ocean delicacy. In those magical days every dive was like an Easter egg hunt, always searching for that one tiny spot that had not yet been discovered; virgin is what we called those reefs. Good name.

I suppose that's what this story is really all about, the unparalleled excitement of discovering virgin territory. And whenever that happened I always asked myself, what must the underwater world have looked like when it was all pure? When never a human eye or hand had been cast beneath the churning surface; when all was in perfect order, life upon life, reeling in its fecundity and abundance. What a sight that must have been.

I want to dive Laguna Beach in the year 1492, long before fleets of probing Europeans decimated the seal and sea otter colonies; before the lobster traps, and fish traps, before gill nets, long lines, and purse seine nets; before the word commercial was ever used in conjunction with fishing. I want to return to Laguna Beach to the days after a storm, when twenty-pound lobsters would wash up live on the beach and the Shoshone would gather them up to use for fertilizer.

I'm getting ahead of myself.

Suffice it to say that in such a fantasy one must really have to know a place, like I knew Laguna Beach. I haven't been there now in eleven years. But I could return tomorrow and swim directly out to any one of several score of hidden reefs and feel reasonably certain I could dig out a fish in a specific hole, or a lobster, (undersized no doubt), maybe an abalone or two. The Laguna waters have been generous to me in more ways than providing bounty. Those waters were my school, the University of Laguna Beach, where I majored in Ocean Intuition. No written tests, no oral exams; the school of direct experience.

I was taught how to read a reef and know from the surface if a lobster would be in a certain cave, because of the way it lined up with the surge and prevailing currents, and its proximity to sand or eel grass, or if there was an eddy where sea garbage tended to gather. I learned to find abalone by knowing the kind of seaweed they like to feed on that was near caves which tunneled surges. So many of these signs are buried in my subconscious; signs I could not explain in any other terms but intuition. It is the knowing of the existence of something without ever seeing it. In the end I make my dive expecting to find one thing or another, and, lo and behold, it is usually there.

What I'm getting at in all this is that you have to know the waters like you would know the cherished face of a loved one. Then when you return to 1492, you'll pretty much know where to look, but of course the reefs will be much different, they'll be virgin.

To fully appreciate virginity, one would also have to experience it at one time or another. And in certain respects of course we all have, but in terms of the natural world very few of us have had the opportunity, and those opportunities are becoming scarcer by the day. I have been fortunate enough to have witnessed such purity of wilderness in my lifetime. I can easily recall the first one. (How could one ever forget such a thing?) Cabo San Lucas in 1968 was still a fishing village. We had landed our four-seater plane on the dirt runway, found an American with a good boat and went miles up the Pacific side of Baja on a mild, spring morning. For reasons I have never fully understood, we decided to anchor in this little cove and have a look around. The water was clear as new blown glass, and the sand bottom reflected the high sun. In the middle of this cove, in thirty feet of water stood this rather innocuous reef, nothing much at first glance. And then, coming closer, the reef, green and orange with sharp angels, moved. Lobster. Nearly every inch of rock was covered with lobster. They spilled out onto the sand and were walking around in the broad daylight. They had never seen a man. They were so jammed into one another they couldn't get out of the way when we began to pluck the big ones which ran eight to ten pounds. Then, as if detonated, they would explode at once into great balls of snapping tails and whirling antennae. It was a sight to see.

There have been others. A cave, as big as a man standing, filled with perhaps two hundred abalone. A solitary rock, out in the middle on nowhere, every inch of it loaded with scallops. And fish, enough fish to blind the eye when the sun catches their scales and creates a shimmering wall of light from the ocean floor to the surface. All of it a mere footnote of some great presence that once represented life itself, pulsing and hammering its way into existence, filling every crack and crevice with its fecund power and breathless beauty.

There is something enormously powerful in seeing a piece of the wilderness that you know beyond doubt has never been touched, or set upon by man. I believe it is why men climb mountains. Not because, "the mountains are there," but because the unblemished wilderness holds in its absolute purity the essence of spirituality that man has lost, and the bold ones spend their lives seeking. Ordinary men are left to build grand cathedrals in their feeble attempts to somehow house this lost spiritually. Such power cannot be housed by man. It is held in the hands of what we call the environment. In my lifetime I have seen these hands grow weak and frail, and the magic they once held sifts like sand between the fingers, and man now chokes to death in the dust of his own making.

I want to dive in waters that bear no evidence of man, no aluminum beer cans, no plastic baggies, no floating styrofoam, no dumped batteries, no nuclear waste that leaks unseen into the liquid atmosphere. I want the baptism of pure nature to cleanse me. I want that purity to seep into my skin. I want those moments that men have when they stand on mountain tops, or wander unsullied reefs, or discover some ancient woods that have somehow been avoided. I want to know what it is to be in the presence of the Great Spirit, as the Native Americans called it: to be holy for a moment; to remember that all men, women and children once had this feeling of completeness, and heard the song of life in a wilderness yet untrampled by acculturated man.

I stand with my gear bag over my shoulder in the center of Cress Street. The Hotel California to my right, the Little Shrimp bar and restaurant to my left, the buzzing of bumper to bumper traffic behind me working its way up and down Pacific Coast Highway. Facing the ocean, I look out and over the three breaking reefs, close my eyes and evoke an incantation that removes me from the concept of linear time that I already know is an illusion, a manufactured device to assure man he is indeed standing on solid ground, when he is not. I next evoke the year, which in the time\space continuum is always happening now. Everything is happening NOW.

Silence.

The sounds of the sea grow in volume. The same sea sounds heard moments ago without the discordant murmurs of man and machine. The stillness is all-pervading and seems to give my hearing abnormal power, as if the sound of each centimeter of water that falls to the beach is being registered. The air bites cleanly into my lungs and I open my eyes. The three reefs remain in their place. The road is gone, the Hotel California, and the Little Shrimp are gone. Turning back to the highway there is nothing but the gently rolling hills to the sky. My perspective is slightly different, lower, and nearer the beach. Large oak trees cluster in the creases of the hills and fan out, holding the earth with their roots. The hills have not yet begun to slide towards the sea. The beach is not like the beach of 1992. The sea has cut a sharp cliff that must be carefully navigated. On the beach great mounds of kelp accumulate high against the cliffs, like amber nests of pterodactyls. Bleached bones of what appears to be a whale, pro-trude from the kelpnest, as if the remains of a predator's prey. Molted lobster carcases four and five feet long and a foot and a half across are stacked like cordwood at the base of the mountainous kelp. Broken abalone and clam shells catch the sun and glitter their fate among the ocean debris. Some appear to have been as big as serving platters.

Clouds of fleece, like bottled sunshine, tilt lazily in the ice blue sky. Terns, pelicans, gulls, and shearwaters wheel and fall from the same sky. The pelicans in endless strings, loop, stall and then dive into the surf break. The gulls are quick behind them scarfing up the stunned bait that has been missed by the punch of the pelican. The shearwaters clean the bits and pieces that remain.

Sitting on a boulder I dress for the sea. The surf is low and the gentle waves are translucent. In the crest of a wave there appears the silhouette of a school of fish rendered visible in the moment of the wave.

With gear in place I walk to the small surfline then lay into the water, kicking past the break. Corbina, white as the sand, and two and a half feet long scatter in the shallow water at my shadow. On both sides of me the corbina pool like liquid platinum, so dense they have trouble getting out of each others way. In eight feet of water two spider crabs, with bodies the size of hubcaps wrestle with a morsel. Beyond the spider crabs halibut lay beneath schooling anchovies. Suddenly the halibut lifts and snags the bait which explodes like sliver shrapnel. Several of the anchovies are wounded in the attack and flounder to the sand. From a nearby rock appear the antennae and then the body of a lobster nearly fifteen pounds. It beats the spider crabs to the fish and brings it deftly to its mouth with forelegs as big as my wrists. I dive to a rock that is the beginning of an outcropping. Every crack and crevice is crammed with lobster, antennae waver and sense the vibrations of the sea like a prehistoric sea anemone. They do not back away from me; they have no fear. A big bull emerges from my left, from antenna to tail it is six feet long, and moves toward me intent on battle. I must look like another lobster in size and awkwardness, and so back away to return to the surface.

A hundred feet from shore I am engulfed in a cloud of bait fish. It takes a moment to recognize that they are sardines; wiped off the face of California waters by commercial fisherman during the 1940s and 50s. Among the sardines are anchovies and spanish mackerel. Together the huge school moves as a single, jade-green entity, stretching from the surface to the sea floor. Their twitching bodies flashing sliver from white underbellies like a wall of neon that blinks out undecipherable messages. I dive and the school separates like a thick cloak shifting in an uncertain wind. After passing through, the cloak folds behind me, sealing off the light, save for the neon that is now twinkling like a new-born galaxy in deep space. On the sand more halibut. I count over twenty in fifty square feet. Another rock outcropping and deep within its cracks lay monster abalone. While I wonder why they are not covering every inch of rock and reef, I see, or rather feel a movement to my right, and zipping beneath me a sea otter, sleek as a furry arrow. I had forgotten about the sea otter and how they roamed from Mexico to Canada before the turn of the twentieth century, and how they were very nearly wiped out by man in his quest for pelts. So it is the sea otter that has kept the abalone population at bay. They dart around me now in two's and three's, curious, almost friendly, sniffing my fins then shooting off whenever I make a movement.

Between the second and third reefs the kelp is thick and difficult to penetrate. I dive beneath it and calico bass scatter by the hundreds, some appear to weigh fifteen pounds. Coming up again, I make a hole in the kelp with my hands to push my head through so that I can get a breath. Another dive, and as I near the outside edge of the kelp, I stop short; for filtering through the golden forest of kelp trees, in still relatively shallow water, drift white sea bass; big and round like old trees at the trunk. How grand they are, like silver ghosts that are so many they light the water with their reflected incandescence. I have forgotten my breath, and hold suspended in the kelp. The school is unending, and when finally I must surface I still have not seen its end. My movement spooks them, not so much into flight, there are so many, hundreds, perhaps thousands, but in a shift from my presence. Now they surround me in curiosity, and with a full breath again I sink among them. All is silver light, moving from every corner of my eye. I am overcome, moved by the absolute power of the natural world displaying its artistry. It's as if all the power in the universe were captured in these grand fish; in their numbers as well as in their size. I am uplifted, as if by being in the company of great beings, I too have achieved greatness. I realize it is not greatness, though that is what I feel, but connectedness to the fish, to nature, to the planet, to all that lives and glows with life. My body tingles as if small currents of electricity were running in and out of my finger tips, eyes, and solar plexus. The white sea bass have included me, have taken me into their tribe. In this moment I am the white sea bass, and reflect my own light. I lift like the rays of light to the surface, unaware of breaths, but breathing. The school finally passes, and I scarcely feel my body.

Transfixed, I wander to the third reef where a school of yellowtail, all big, all over fifty pounds, breeze by. Bold and unafraid, one spots me on the surface and rises to investigate. The others follow and the water boils on the surface with their cutting fins as they circle. I am dizzy from the spectacular display.

Behind the yellows come the bonito in bullet spreads at high speed, shredding a large school of wandering barracuda that re-groups after the bonito have thundered by. A little further out, where lies a significant drop-off, I suspect bluefin and yellowfin tuna, and who knows what else would be churning by. My thoughts flick to the future and in the enormous loss never realized by my human family, and in that instant I have muddled with the forces of the time\space continuum. The sound of a distant outboard engine whines from somewhere. The kelp has thinned considerably and there is no sign of fish, of life, save for a single senorita fish, hiding beneath a kelp leaf. We are alone, this fish and I. The hills glitter with the glass of homes and there are sunbathers on the beach. The air smells of exhaust fumes. The magical connection to the ocean and the planet that I felt moments ago, seeps away like blood from an open wound.

Slowly I make my way back to the beach where I must encounter my own time. There is no hurry. I am bleeding. The planet is bleeding. For the first time I recognize the faintness of its heart beat. My own heart has lost its vigor, as if all that is the energy of life that had run through me moments before has vanished, leaving me shriveled and dry, nearly finished.

Reaching the beach I stand to look at the three reefs that pro-trude through the water as they did five hundred years ago, and as they will five hundred years from now. And I wonder what will be left in five hundred years? Anything at all?

c. e.
summer of '91

The Way of the Dolphin, the Way of Man

W HY DO DOLPHINS EVOKE such powerful feelings in us? There are books of every kind regarding the subject. They cover topics ranging from psychotherapy to dreams, from child-birthing to metaphysical channeling. I doubt there is a subject of mystical interest in the human experience that is not covered somewhere in a book about dolphins.

One does not have to look far for an explanation. Our lives, and the substance of the society we created has run amok. We have serious difficulties with values, relationships and family. Our young, improperly nourished, on all fronts, run wild in the streets. We have replaced our sense of play with a work ethic that borders on maniacal. We are spiritually impoverished and have forgotten how to live well. Really live, in the sense of understanding and participating in the full spectrum of life, of following our bliss, and of trusting in the perfection of the universe. Don't get me wrong, we want to do these things. We, at some level, understand our compass has broken and have drifted way off course, but because we are fragmented we don't know which way to turn the ship. We are in search of a captain that can lead us home again.

More than at any time in this millennium people are seeking answers, trying to make sense of the dilemma in which they find themselves.

It was not always so. Long ago and not very far away the earth overflowed with mystery. Nature dominated and man had to look to the shaman or medicine woman for guidance in matters of love, health, family, and social values. The shaman and medicine women were able to move into realms of knowledge that were inaccessible to members of the tribe. They were content to simply be connected to the greater wisdom of the earth by living humbly in balance and harmony with their surroundings. The answers brought back from the Other World by the shaman were consistent with the life-style being led and thus were of value. And even though the shaman might speak to stones or listen to trees, or see visions, the laws under which everyone lived were whole and unfragmented, and, most importantly, they made sense. And so it was for several million years.

Eventually that knowledge was wiped out by a different kind of priest. Ones who came from different lands with different laws. Ones who were more interested in power and control than in the balance and harmony.

The damage done was unremitting and total. Great knowledge was lost. The tribal peoples of the earth were betrayed under the cloak of new religion. One that came from outside nature and did not address fundamental understandings about the way things worked. It was the beginning of the end for balance and harmony.

The final blow was delivered with the arrival of still another religion, the one we call science. Science had in its collective mind to redefine the natural world. To unearth all the mystery and reveal it to the cold eye of the microscope. And so it came to pass. They reduced what was once whole into kingdoms, phyla, classes, orders, families, genera, and species. They reduced and divided until there was nothing left but protons and neutrons. In the doing they discovered that the world could not be dissected into pieces and fragments and still be clearly defined. They discovered that the observer influenced the observed. They discovered that everything is connected. We are all connected. We are connected to each other. We are connected to nature. We are connected to the planet. They discovered what the shaman had always known.

Unfortunately, knowing, that is the intellectual knowing, is not enough. Such stuff is merely information, not knowledge. As any good shaman knows, true knowledge must be acquired through the direct experience. Something three dimensional, (not through the television), something the body and spirit can experience as well as the mind. We often confuse information with knowledge.

These days we intuitively desire someone who understands the whole, unfragmented world, and can help fix us and our broken society. We are looking for a shaman, or medicine woman to listen to the trees and tell us how to find our way back home again. Back to balance and harmony, back to following our personal bliss, back to trusting in the perfection of the universe, back to the joy of play. There are many pretenders to the throne, but none have been able to bear close examination. It is easy to deceive desperate people. So we continue to look for the true sage. One who is mysterious. One who holds obvious secrets. One who's language, whether primitive or advanced, can reveal to us lost knowledge. One from a tribe whose wisdom has remained intact.

Enter the dolphin into late twentieth-century consciousness.

The dolphin embodies all that humans have discarded; all that humans have lost. They live in large families, they play, they make love, they operate out of truth. (Their sonar can "read" an entire bio-physical system in a micro-second. When the truth is not spoken that system changes, thus they can immediately distinguish a lie from the truth. (But of course they don't have to.) Their society works. It has stood the test of time for thirty million years.

It is no wonder so many books are written to feed the desperate longing in ourselves to live in such a society. And why we so relent-lessly pursue them in the obscure hope we can learn something and change the direction of our lives, maybe even change our society.

I was not trying to change my life when I encountered dolphins last week. I don't believe a dolphin, or a priest, or a scientist, or a politician can change my life, or change the society in which I am living. I know I can make changes in my life and thus in my society. I am the shaman, the priest, the scientist all rolled into one. We all are. I search for answers in myself. I was not trying to find those answers when I swam with the dolphins last week. It was the last thing on my mind. I wanted to take photographs of those marvelous creatures. But something happened.

There is a single place in the world where wild dolphins will interact with man. (I have learned by rumor that there is another such place somewhere in Indonesian waters, but until confirmed it remains a rumor.) These dolphin are not enticed by food or favors of any kind. They join man of their own free will, and they leave of their own free will. This special place lies on a sizeable sand bank in the

Bahamas and has been the source of dolphin encounters for nearly twenty years.

At one time the place of the dolphins was a secret, but no more, the charter boats out of Fort Lauderdale, Florida know their way out to the sand bank, some fifty miles from land, but only one boat, the *Dream Too,* and its skipper, Scott Smith, know it better than anyone else. It was on this vessel that ten underwater photographers from all over the world, including Australians Barry Andrewartha and Kelvin Aitken and Jim Watt from Hawaii, headed out for a week on the sand bank.

Photographers are no different than anyone else in society. They know there is a dolphin consciousness and so they fill the demands of society with their photographs. However, to a man, I did not observe any of them seeking answers to questions plaguing the rest of society. Only the skipper, Scott Smith raised a lofty question. He did this indirectly during the orientation meeting when we were still at the dock. He placed unusual emphasis on violation of the dolphin's world. "If they don't want us, we will not force it," is what he said in effect. At the time no one was paying much attention. Photographers are an aggressive lot. They were gambling a lot of money on this trip, and by God they were going to get some pictures, whether the dolphin liked it or not. Scott knew better, he had done this hundreds of times. He knew much more than he was letting on.

The first day on the banks we did not spot dolphin until late in the afternoon. The dolphins were swift and the water never deeper than thirty five feet so free diving was the optimum method for encounter. It soon became obvious that the best swimmers and free divers would get the best pictures. Everyone was competing and showing little courtesy to slower divers, much less to the dolphins themselves. Almost immediately the dolphins began to wander off with the pack of photographers in futile pursuit.

In swept Scott on an underwater scooter, on a breath-hold, doing turns and loops and twists to catch the dolphin's attention and bring them back to the pursuing photographers. One of us caught on right away; Camp, who was not a professional photographer, abandoned the camera and began to dolphin-kick down and mimic the dolphin's movements. The dolphin immediately responded, and swam over to Camp and engaged him in dolphin play while the rest of us burned rolls of film. It was chiefly through the efforts of Camp and Scott that the dolphin remained interested and stuck around. After an exhausting fifty minutes that had us jelly-legged, and gasping, the dolphins grew weary of their sluggish friends and disappeared into the glycerine sea.

While the rest of us babbled on about the shots made and missed, Camp sat by himself in the corner of the boat. "You really got in there among them," I said. "What was it like?"

"I can't really say," he said smiling. "It was incredible. I can't explain it."

Camp is a physician by trade, and doctors generally have explanations for everything. This was a curious departure from my experience. However, at the time it went unregistered. I was too involved with photography to realize that perhaps he had been affected by the dolphins in a meaningful way.

The following day we had five separate encounters. For the most part Camp and Scott swam with the dolphins, imitated their movements, and were accepted into the "water space" the dolphins occupied. At one time Scott, employing his dolphin kick, swam alongside one dolphin when four others came in and enclosed him on all sides, and they all swam as one; members of the same pod. It was a spectacular sight to behold. Not spectacular, that is a photographer's word. It was a wondrous sight. As if one had come upon a meadow in a deep forest and found a man milling about with a herd of wild deer. It defied logic. Obviously some sort of contact was going on. Some form of communication was at play. But what? Later, I asked Scott if he could enlighten me. He smiled, "No," he said. "I have no words for it. It's beyond words. Beyond thought. It's like something familiar. But its so deep you can't bring it up."

It was clear I was missing something important. On the last encounter, which occurred in the middle of our dinner at six thirty in the evening, I jumped in the water with photography second on the priority list.

There were four dolphin in the pod. I had recognized one from yesterday. The one Scott called Chopper, who was easily identifiable by a crescent bite, from a shark no doubt, out of his dorsal fin. I dropped down using a dolphin kick. Chopper immediately broke away from his mates and joined me — swimming alongside my right side less than feet away. The speckled, silver body glowed in the low light and its eye, astonishing human-like when seen up-close, gazed at me sleepily. I turned on my back and continued to kick at an angle towards the bottom. Chopper moved closer, swimming inches away; we were belly-to-belly, looking directly into the other's eyes. Scott said it is the only position where the dolphin can see a subject with both eyes. They make love in the same position.

The contact brought about a pleasant feeling. One that is difficult to describe. Light, and warm, as if I was being mildly hypnotized. There was intelligence in the eyes, a depth of knowledge that I did not possess, could not possess, or had once possessed and had lost. All these thoughts, and ideas of what was taking place came to me later. At the time, in the moment, my mind was without thought, blissfully quiet.

An invitation was extended.

I placed my hand on the white chest inches away. It felt smooth as newborn skin. My heart slowed and then quickened as if in the first touch of the beloved's hand on the first date with the woman you know you will marry; powerful, exciting, dizzying.

We bent together and rose as one to the surface. There the connection was broken, and Chopper drifted off. (Scott informed me that Chopper was one of only three dolphins of the eighty with which he was familiar that allowed any kind of touching. Later I tried to touch other dolphin and they would simply move out of reach. Even when I was just inches away they could feel me reaching. I managed to sneak a touch to the side of one dolphin and was promptly smacked on the side of my head with a tail.)

I dived again and Chopper picked me up half-way to the bottom. I could see his eye clearly. The pupil was dark, and the lid was shaded in brown. The eye was wide, very human. There came the feeling, (not a thought), of something from the eye that passed between us. In my ignorance; the ignorance of the tamed and fragmented; the ignorance of the civilized; the message went uncomprehended. The eye, like that of a shaman who knows only the truth, patiently waited for me to understand. I was drawn inexorably into the eye, into the unnamed thing that was being given to me. That was touching me in some primordial place that laid beyond, behind, or buried deep inside my civilized constructs. The entire episode was unfolding like a wonderful dream, one in which I was not the dreamer, but the dreamed.

I knew not of the water, or my breath-hold, or of the depth I was swimming. I was filled with the wise, dark eye brimming with knowledge. A knowledge that had a vague familiarity, like a whiff of untamed smoke hovering in the belly. I reached out and slid my hand along Chopper's side, like the lover who is searching for the hand of his bride. I wanted to embrace Chopper with both arms, wrap my legs around him. Just a flash of desire. Chopper broke off his swim and abandoned me. The bond was broken.

I wanted too much; the undoing of civilized man.

I cannot exactly say what went on during those moments with Chopper. Scott cautioned it was important not to think when swimming with the dolphins. Thinking ruins everything, he said. Thinking just gets in the way.

I believe the dolphin understood my longing for its wisdom. It could feel my need and so did not turn away. The unsaid passes before us all the time in our human world. And we are able to identify much of it. We know, for example, the look of anger, fear, love, and hate. But what does the long steady gaze of a wild creature express? We mis-use the word wild, for many it has a negative connotation. I prefer untamed or uncivilized (they are sadly synonymous). This look from the untamed eye had no anger, no fear, no hate. The look I later came up with was wise, and dare I say it without sounding corny, love. It was also the look that comes from the supremely confident. Of one who knows not so much the world but knows himself clearly, without a trace of fear or self doubt. I long to look in a mirror and find those same aspects in myself.

I cannot say if dolphins are more intelligent than humans. They have been around thirty million years longer than humans, and that has to count for something. Particularly considering our five million year history, which, if we continue upon our present path, will bring us well short of that mark.

Dolphins exist in a pure reality that is without deception or illusion. I believe that because of their ability with sonar and echo location to "read' the inner terrain of life forms, that the truth is immediately recognized and all else is dismissed. Thus without anger, hatred, fear, deception or illusion they exist in a reality unlike our own. With that in mind one must ponder what sort of mind or more accurately, what sort of state-of-being could develop in that kind of environment? We may never know.

I know that for a moment the darkness that shrouds the civilized man fell away in the light of a dolphin's eye. Ever so briefly the shaman spoke. But alas, I was unable to understand the message. I must become my own shaman, and find my own truths. Become confident in the wisdom that truth will bring, and know myself fully, without doubt. I have come to realize that this is the message of the dolphin; to serve as examples of what life might be like existing on such a plane.

c.e   fall '92

OTHER TITLES BY WATERSPORT BOOKS

DEEP DIVING
An Advanced Guide to Physiology Procedures and Systems
by Bret Gilliam and Robert von Maier

DRY SUIT DIVING
A Guide to Diving Dry
by Steve Barsky, Dick Long, and Bob Stinton

NIGHT DIVING
A Consumer's Guide to the Specialty of Night Diving
by Ken Loyst

WHEN WOMEN DIVE
A Female's Guide to Both Diving and Snorkeling
By Erin O'Neill and Ella Jean Morgan

DIVE COMPUTERS
A Consumer's Guide to History, Theory, and Performance
By Ken Loyst

MIXED GAS DIVING
The Ultimate Challenge For Technical Diving
by Tom Mount and Bret Gilliam

SOLO DIVING
The Art of Underwater Self-Sufficiency
by Robert von Maier

SEA SHADOWS
In-Depth Perspectives of Nature
By Carlos Eyles

SECRET SEAS
Stories and Essays of the Sea
by Carlos Eyles

HAWAI'I BELOW
Favorites, Tips and Secrets of the Diving Professionals
by Rod Canham

THE EGYPTIAN RED SEA
A Diver's Guide
by Eric Hanauer

DIVING FREE by Carlos Eyles
LAST OF THE BLUE WATER HUNTERS by Carlos Eyles
THE AMBER FOREST by Ron McPeak, Dale Glantz, and Carol Shaw

WATERSPORT BOOKS
A Division of: Watersport Publishing, Inc.
P.O. Box 83727, San Diego, CA 92138 • (619) 697-0703 or Fax (619) 697-0123